JERSEY SCHOLAR'S

500

MATH

PRACTICE
QUESTIONS
FOR THE

SAT TEST

Scott Goodman

Jersey Scholar LLC

Jersey Scholar LLC
Bloomfield, NJ 07003
Email: scott@jerseyscholar.com

ISBN-13: 979-8-218-02233-4

TABLE OF CONTENTS

QUESTIONS & ANSWERS

Can I use a calculator for the questions in this book? Yes, this book was designed to be completed with a calculator.

Why do some questions have no answer choices? On the real SAT, almost one quarter of the questions have no answer choices. Instead, you'll provide your own answer and fill in bubbles to provide that response. This book mostly contains questions with answers choices, but almost one quarter will not.

Are there math formulas provided on the SAT? Yes. The same geometry reference information that is given at the beginning of every SAT math section is provided at the beginning of the geometry chapter of this book, chapter 7.

How long should it take me to complete a chapter? To be at the speed required to finish an SAT test in the allotted amount of time, you should be able to complete the 50 questions in a chapter in about an hour.

Does this book cover every topic that will be found on the SAT? While we can't know for sure what will be on a future SAT, this book covers virtually every math topic seen on past released SATs.

Why are there no scoring tables in this book? The questions in this book are ordered by topic, so they do not accurately mimic a real SAT and should not be used to estimate a future score.

What if I have a question? Please reach out to us! We'd be happy to help if you have any questions or comments. Please email us at scott@jerseyscholar.com.

Linear Equations

1.

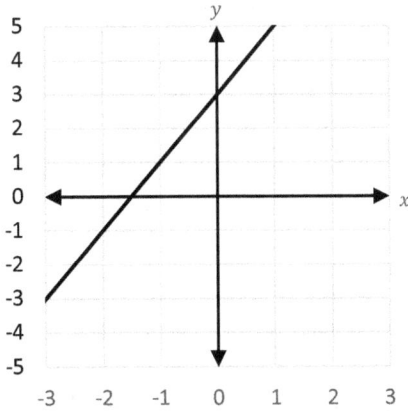

The graph of the linear function $f(x) = mx + 3$ is shown in the xy-plane, where m is a constant. What is the value of m?

A) -2

B) -1

C) 1

D) 2

2.

The graph of $y = \frac{4}{3}x - 5$ in the xy-plane is a line. What is the slope of the line?

3.

What is the y-intercept of the line in the xy-plane with equation $y = -3x + 2$?

4.

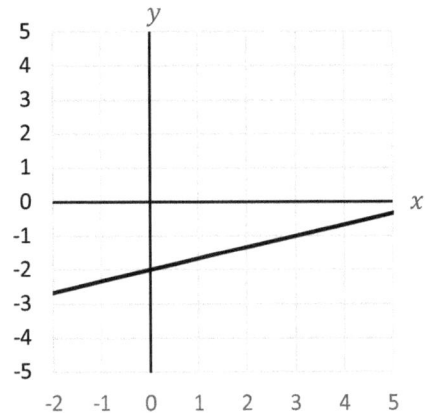

Which of the following is an equation of the graph shown?

A) $y = 3x - 2$

B) $y = 3x + 6$

C) $y = \frac{1}{3}x - 2$

D) $y = \frac{1}{3}x + 6$

5.

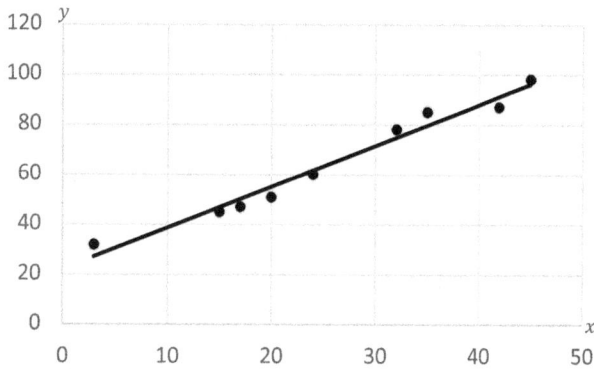

A data set of 9 points is shown in the scatterplot. A line of best fit for the data is also shown. For how many of the data points is the y-value predicted by the line of best fit less than the actual y-value?

A) 3

B) 4

C) 5

D) 6

6.

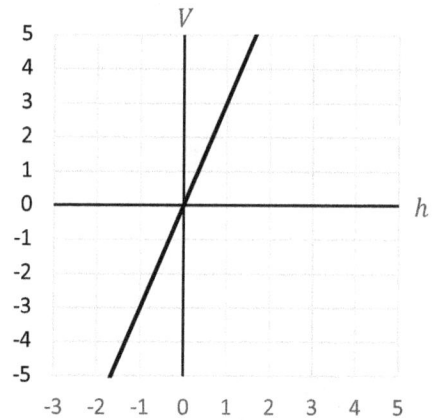

A group of rectangular prisms that has a fixed length l and width w, in centimeters, each has a height h, in centimeters, and volume V, in cubic centimeters. The graph shows the relationship between some values of h and V. Which of the following equations best represents this relationship?

A) $V = h + 3$

B) $V = h + \frac{1}{3}$

C) $V = 2h$

D) $V = 3h$

7.

On a car trip, Carl drove east on a straight highway and noted the distance travelled at various times during his trip. The scatterplot below shows these distances as a function of the time since the start of his trip. A line of best fit is also shown.

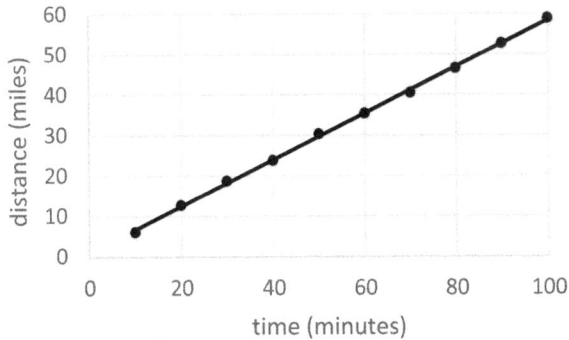

Which of the following is best approximation of the equation of the line of best fit shown, where d is the distance, in miles, and t is the time, in minutes, since the trip began?

A) $d = \frac{1}{2}t$

B) $d = t$

C) $d = \frac{3}{2}t$

D) $d = 2t$

8.

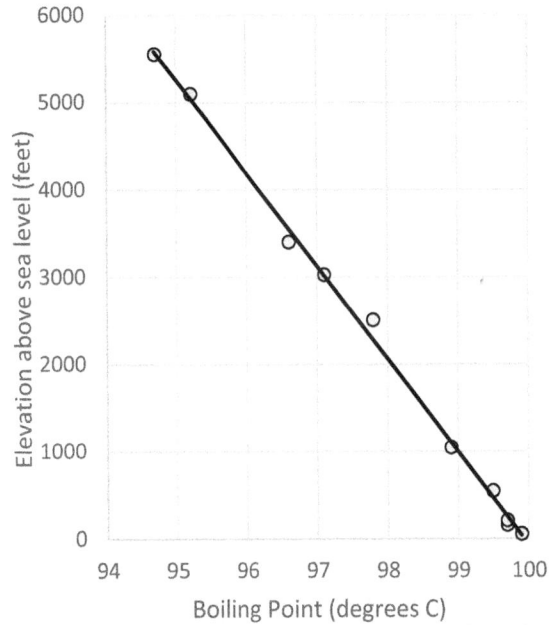

The scatterplot above shows the actual measured boiling point, in degrees Celsius, at 11 different elevations. A line of best fit is also shown. When the elevation was 2500 feet above sea level, how much greater was the actual boiling point, in degrees Celsius, than the boiling point predicted by the line of best fit?

A) .025

B) .25

C) 2.5

D) 250

9.

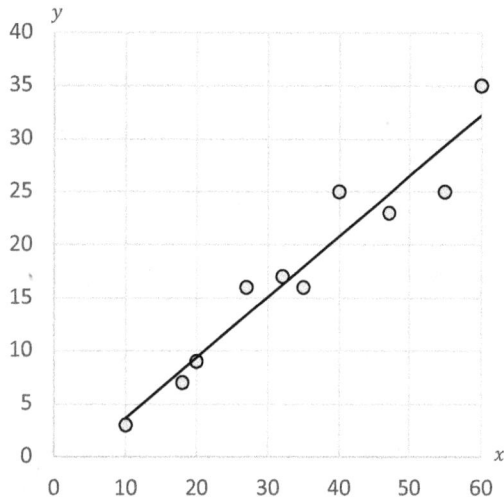

The scatterplot shows a data set of 10 points and a line of best fit for the data. For how many of the data points is the y-value predicted by the line of best fit less than the actual y-value?

10.

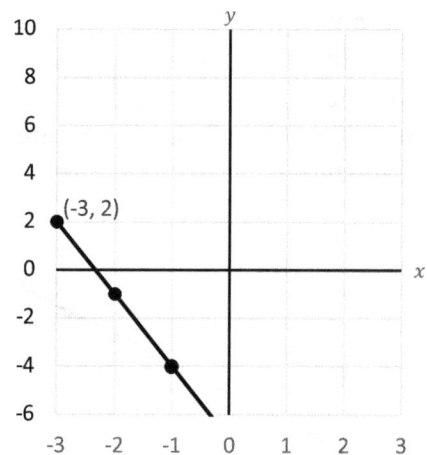

The graph of a line in the xy-plane is shown above. What is the equation that defines this line?

A) $y = -3x - 3$

B) $y = -3x - 7$

C) $y = 3x - 3$

D) $y = 3x - 7$

11.

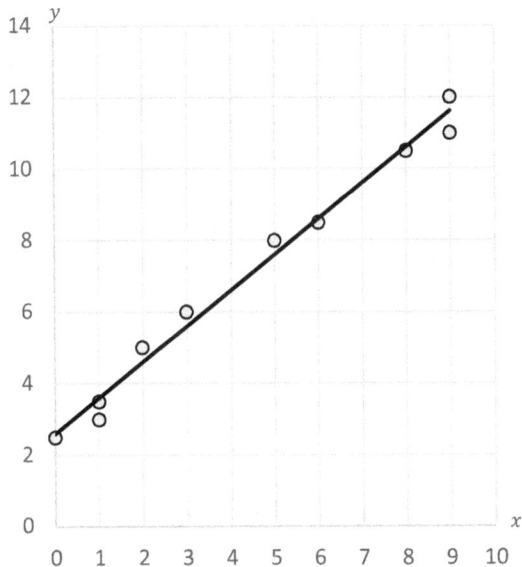

The scatterplot above shows a relationship between two variables, x and y. What is an equation of the line of best fit?

A) $y = x + 2.5$

B) $y = 2.5x + 1$

C) $y = x - 2.5$

D) $y = 2.5x - 1$

12.

In the xy-plane, the equation of the line containing the points $(2, 3)$ and $(4, 5)$ can be written in the form $y = mx + b$, where m and b are constants. What is the value of m?

13.

x	-3.0	-1.0	1.0	2.0	5.0
$f(x)$	2.5	-2.5	-7.5	-10.0	-17.5

The table above shows some values of a variable x and the corresponding values of the function $f(x)$. Which of the following equations could represent the relationship between x and $f(x)$?

A) $f(x) = \frac{5}{2}x - 5$

B) $f(x) = -5x + 5$

C) $f(x) = -5x - 5$

D) $f(x) = -\frac{5}{2}x - 5$

14.

A line in the xy-plane has a slope of -2 and passes through the point $(1, 2)$. Which is an equation of the line?

A) $y = -2x$

B) $y = -2x + 2$

C) $y = -2x + 4$

D) $y = -2x + 6$

15.

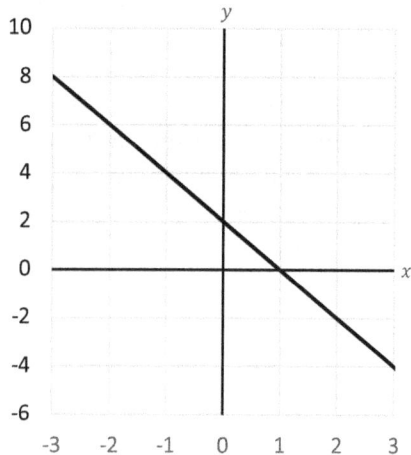

Line q is shown above in the xy-plane. Which of the following is an equation of a perpendicular line to line q that passes through the point (-1, 0)?

A) $y = x + 2$

B) $y = x + 1$

C) $y = \frac{1}{2}x + 1$

D) $y = \frac{1}{2}x + \frac{1}{2}$

16.

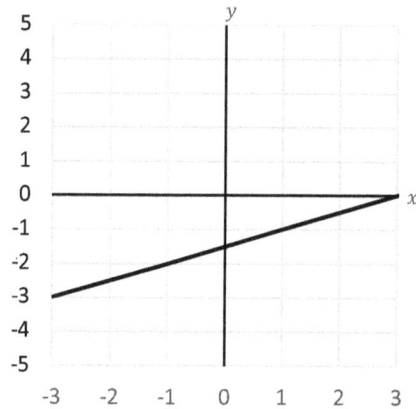

Line m is shown in the xy-plane above. Which of the following is an equation of a line perpendicular to line m?

A) $y = -\frac{1}{2}x + 3$

B) $y = \frac{1}{2}x - \frac{3}{2}$

C) $y = 2x + 3$

D) $y = -2x + 3$

17.

The graph of the equation $2y + 3x = n$, where n is a constant, is a line in the xy-plane. Which of the following are the coordinates of the y-intercept of the graph?

A) $(0, \frac{n}{3})$

B) $(0, \frac{n}{2})$

C) $(0, -\frac{n}{3})$

D) $(0, -\frac{n}{2})$

18.

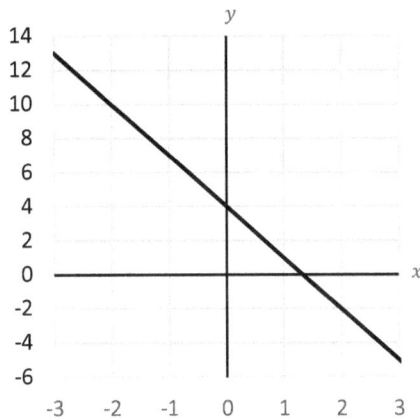

Line n is shown in the xy-plane above. Which of the following is an equation of line n?

A) $3x + y = 4$

B) $3x - y = 4$

C) $x + 3y = 4$

D) $x - 3y = 4$

19.

In the xy-plane, line l can be defined by the equation $y = mx + b$, where m and b are constants, and passes through the point $(-3, 2)$. If line m is parallel to line l and can be defined by the equation $y = \frac{4}{3}x - 5$, what is the value of b?

20.

A builder has completed 65 homes in a neighborhood by March. The equation $h = 65 + 6t$ gives the total number of homes, h, in the neighborhood t months after March. Which of the following is the best interpretation of the number 6 in the context of this equation?

A) The total number of homes completed after t months

B) The increase in the number of homes each month

C) The initial number of homes in the neighborhood in March

D) The number of months it will take to complete h homes

21.

In the xy-plane, the graph of $y = 3x + b$, where b is a constant, intersects the x-axis at the point $(-2, 0)$. What is the value of b?

22.

Line n in the xy-plane has equation $y = \frac{2}{3}x + 5$. Line p is perpendicular to line n and passes through the point $(0, -5)$. Which is an equation for line p?

A) $y = -\frac{3}{2}x + 5$

B) $y = -\frac{3}{2}x - 5$

C) $y = -\frac{2}{3}x - 5$

D) $y = \frac{3}{2}x - 5$

23.

The function h is defined by $h(x) = \frac{3}{4}x - 6$. What is the x coordinate of the x-intercept of the graph of $y = h(x)$ in the xy-plane?

24.

What is the y-intercept of the graph with equation $2x + 3y = -6$ in the xy-plane?

A) $(0, -\frac{2}{3})$

B) $(0, -2)$

C) $(-\frac{2}{3}, 0)$

D) $(-2, 0)$

25.

For the linear function f, $f(1) = 7$ and the graph of $y = f(x)$ in the xy-plane has a slope of 4. Which of the following is an equation of the function f?

A) $f(x) = x + 7$

B) $f(x) = 4x + 7$

C) $f(x) = 4x + 11$

D) $f(x) = 4x + 3$

26.

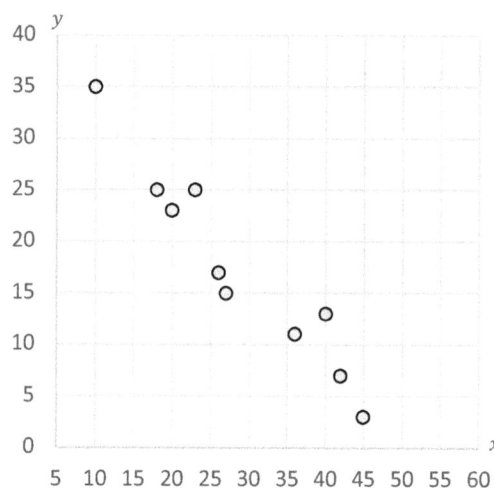

A set of data is shown by the scatterplot in xy-plane above. Which of the following equations best models the data?

A) $y = 35 + .5x$

B) $y = 50 + .8x$

C) $y = 30 - 1.2x$

D) $y = 40 - .8x$

27.

Richie picked 3 tomatoes from his garden today. He estimates that every day this week he will be able to pick 2 more tomatoes than he did the previous day. Which of the following functions f can Richie use to estimate the number of tomatoes he'll be able to pick n days from now?

A) $f(n) = 3n - 2$

B) $f(n) = 2n - 3$

C) $f(n) = 3n + 2$

D) $f(n) = 2n + 3$

28.

x	y
-2	4
2	12

The table shows two values of x and the corresponding value of y that represent two points on a line in the xy-plane. What is the slope of the line?

29.

In the xy-plane, the graph of the linear function f contains the points $(1, 3)$ and $(3, -1)$. Which of the following defines f?

A) $y = -x + 4$

B) $y = 2x + 1$

C) $y = -2x + 5$

D) $y = -2x + 3$

30.

During the first week of the read-a-thon, students at the high school read 154 books combined. From weeks 2 to 6, the number of combined books read each week was 24 books more than the preceding week. Which of the following best approximates the number of books, $b(x)$, read x weeks after the first week of the read-a-thon?

A) $b(x) = 154x + 24$

B) $b(x) = 24 + x$

C) $b(x) = 154 + x$

D) $b(x) = 154 + 24x$

31.

Which of the following pairs of lines represents a system of equations that has no solution?

A) $y = 2x - 3$
$\quad 4x + 2y = -3$

B) $y = 2x + 3$
$\quad 4x - 2y = -6$

C) $y = -2x - 3$
$\quad 4x + 2y = 6$

D) $y = -2x + 3$
$\quad 4x - 2y = 6$

32.

A line in the xy-plane contains the points $(a, \ 4)$ and $(-a, -2)$, where a is a positive constant. If the line is defined by the equation $y = mx + b$, where m and b are constants, what is the value of b?

A) 1

B) 2

C) 3

D) 4

33.

A botanist randomly selects a sample of 10 of a certain variety of tomato. The scatterplot below shows the diameters and masses for the sample of tomatoes, as well as a line of best fit. The equation of the line of best fit is $y = 0.9x - 4.7$

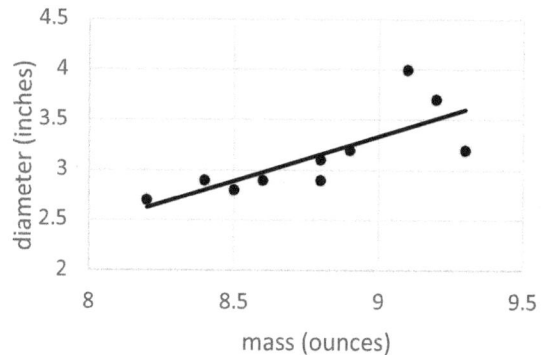

What is the meaning of the slope, 0.9, in this context?

A) The diameter of a tomato is expected to increase 0.9 inches for every 1 ounce increase in mass.

B) The mass is expected to increase 0.9 ounces for every 1 inch increase in diameter.

C) The diameter of a tomato is expected to decrease 0.9 inches for every 1 ounce increase in mass.

D) The mass is expected to decrease 0.9 ounces for every 1 inch increase in diameter.

34.

The graph of the equation $ax + by = 4$ is a line in the xy-plane, where a and b are constants. If the line contains the points $(2, 3)$ and $(0, -3)$, what is the value of b?

A) $-\frac{4}{3}$

B) -1

C) 2

D) 3

35.

In the xy-plane, line j has a slope of $\frac{2}{3}$. Line k is perpendicular to line j and contains the point $(2, 3)$. Which of the following is an equation of line k?

A) $y = \frac{3}{2}x$

B) $y = -\frac{2}{3}x + \frac{13}{3}$

C) $y = -\frac{3}{2}x + 6$

D) $y = -\frac{3}{2}x + 2$

36.

The linear function f in the xy-plane passes through the points $(-2, 4)$ and $(3, 3)$. Which of the following equations defines f?

A) $f(x) = \frac{1}{5}x + \frac{12}{5}$

B) $f(x) = -5x + 18$

C) $f(x) = 5x - 12$

D) $f(x) = -\frac{1}{5}x + \frac{18}{5}$

37.

One of the two equations in a linear system has equation $y = 2x - 3$. The system has no solution. Which could be the other equation in this linear system?

A) $y = \frac{1}{2}x - 3$

B) $y = 2x - 3$

C) $y = 2x - 4$

D) $y = -\frac{1}{2}x - 3$

38.

A real estate agent estimates that the price of a $350,000 house will increase by $10,000 each year after 2020. Which of the following models the price, $p(x)$, in <u>thousands</u> of dollars, of the house t years after 2020?

A) $p(x) = 350 + 10t$

B) $p(x) = 10 + 350t$

C) $p(x) = 350 + 10000t$

D) $p(x) = 10000 - 350t$

39.

The graph of a line in the xy-plane with equation $y = \frac{2}{3}x - 2$ is translated three units to the right. What is the y-intercept of the translated line?

A) 0

B) -2

C) -4

D) -6

40.

x	$f(x)$
2	42
4	82
6	122

The table above gives several values of x and their corresponding values of $f(x)$. The function f is defined by $y = ax + b$, where a and b are constants. What is the value of b?

41.

Height (feet)	Cost (millions of $)
915	925
1050	1015
1200	1115

The table gives some values of the heights h, in feet, of several tall buildings and their corresponding costs to build, c, in millions of dollars. Which of the following equations models this relationship?

A) $c = \frac{2}{3}h + 315$

B) $c = \frac{3}{2}h + 285$

C) $c = -\frac{2}{3}h + 630$

D) $c = -\frac{3}{2}h + 570$

42.

For a linear function f in the xy-plane with graph of $y = f(x)$ and a slope of 2, $f(4) = -2$. Which of the following points lies on the graph of $y = f(x)$?

A) (6, -1)

B) (3, 0)

C) (6, 2)

D) (2, -3)

43.

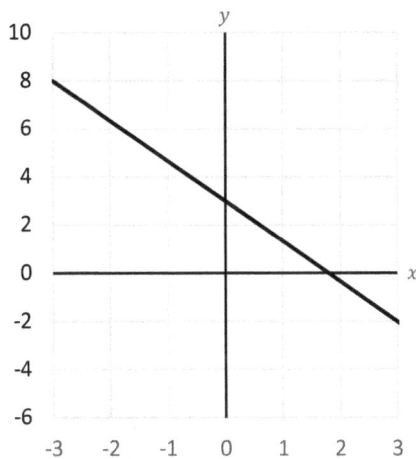

The line above in the xy-plane passes through the points (-3, 8) and (3, -2). It also passes through the point (-1, b). What is the value of b?

44.

The function p is defined by $p(x) = cx + d$, where c and d are constants. If $p(3) = 12$ and $p(5) = 20$, what is the value of d?

45.

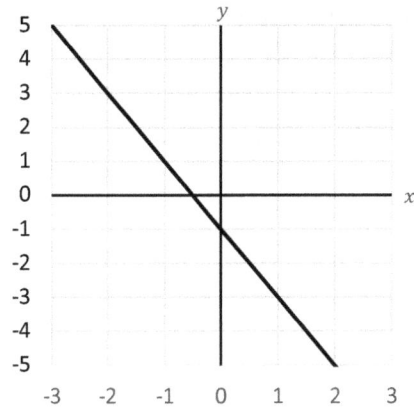

The graph with equation $6x + 3y + C = 0$ where C is a constant, is shown in the xy-plane. What is the value of C?

A) -3

B) -1

C) 2

D) 3

46.

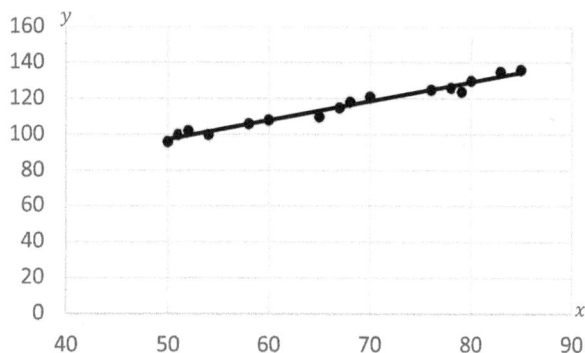

A magazine tested 16 riding lawnmowers. The scatterplot above shows the horsepower x, and the maximum amount mowed in an hour, y, in square yards, for each of the 16 lawnmowers. A line of best fit is also shown. Which of the following could be the equation of the line of best fit?

A) $y = 91 + x$

B) $y = 44 + x$

C) $y = 91 + 5x$

D) $y = 44 + \frac{1}{5}x$

47.

In the xy-plane, a line passes through the points $(-3, 1)$ and $(2, 5)$. If an equation of the line is $y = mx + b$, where m and b are constants, what is the value of b?

48.

x	$h(x)$
2	9
3	6
4	3

For the linear function h, the given table shows several values of x and the corresponding values of $h(x)$. If $h(x) = mx + b$, where m and b are constants, what is the value of b?

A) 5

B) 8

C) 12

D) 15

49.

x	$f(x)$
-5	-13
-2	-7
3	3
5	7

For the linear function f, the table shows several values of x and their corresponding values of $f(x)$. What is the y-intercept of the graph of $f(x)$ in the xy-plane?

A) -3

B) -2

C) -1

D) 0

50.

A balloon will expand and contract with the temperature of the air inside the balloon. The diameter of the balloon $d(T)$, in centimeters, is a linear function of the temperature T, in degrees Fahrenheit, of the air inside the balloon. When the air temperature inside the balloon is 70°F, the diameter is 7 centimeters. When the air temperature inside the balloon is 40°F, the diameter is 5.5 centimeters. Which of the following defines the relationship between the air temperature and the diameter of the balloon?

A) $d(T) = \frac{1}{20}(T - 40) + 5.5$

B) $d(T) = \frac{1}{20}(T + 40) - 5.5$

C) $d(T) = 20(T - 40) + 5.5$

D) $d(T) = 20(T + 40) - 5.5$

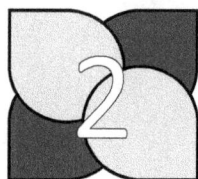

2 Systems of Equations

1.

$$10x - 4y = 22$$
$$y = 12$$

If (x, y) is a solution to the system of equations above, what is the value of x?

2.

Holly has two after school jobs, but only has enough free time to work at most 15 hours in a week. She wants to earn at least $125 this week. At her job as a receptionist, she earns $12 per hour and at her job as a store cashier, she earns $10 per hour. Which of the following systems of inequalities represents this situation, in which r is the number of hours of work as a receptionist and c is the number of hours of work as a cashier?

A) $12r + 10c \leq 125$
$\quad r + c \leq 15$

B) $12r + 10c \geq 125$
$\quad r + c \geq 15$

C) $12r + 10c \geq 125$
$\quad r + c \leq 15$

D) $12r + 10c \geq 15$
$\quad r + c \leq 125$

3.

$$2x + 2y = 4$$
$$2x - 2y = 8$$

If (x, y) is a solution to the system of equations above, what is the value of x?

4.

$$x - y = 2$$
$$3y = 12$$

If (x, y) is the solution to the given system of equations, what is the value of x?

A) 2

B) 4

C) 6

D) 8

5.

$$x = -4$$
$$y = -3x - 12$$

If (x, y) is the solution to the given system of equations, what is the value of y?

6.

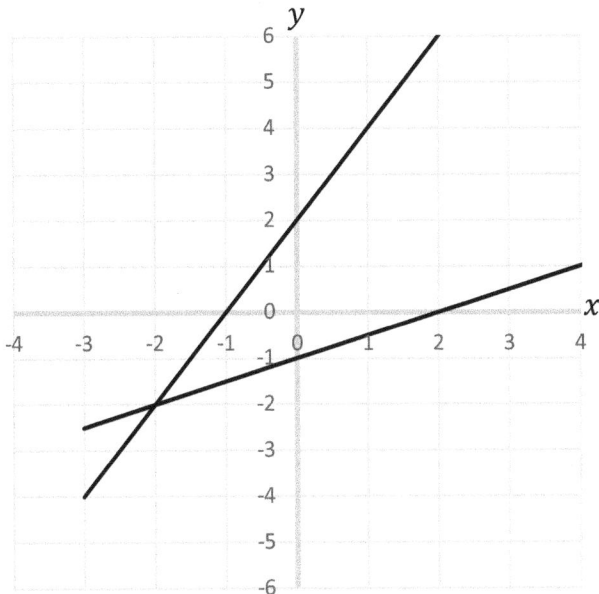

A system of equations is graphed in the xy-plane above. Which of the following points (x, y) represents the solution to this system?

A) (-2, -2)

B) (-2, 2)

C) (-1, 0)

D) (2, 0)

7.

$$y = 3x$$
$$y = 4 - x$$

If (x, y) is the solution to the given system of equations, what is the value of $4x$?

8.

$$x = y + 3$$
$$x = -y + 2$$

The solution to the system of equations above is (x, y). What is the value of x?

A) 1.5

B) 2

C) 2.5

D) 5

9.

$$y = -4x + 2$$
$$y = 4x - 6$$

If the solution to the system of equations above is (x, y), what is the value of $2y$?

A) -4

B) -2

C) 2

D) 4

10.

Maple: $M(t) = 20 + 4t$
Spruce: $S(t) = 5 + 7t$

On April 5th, a maple tree has 20 leaves, and a spruce tree has 5 leaves. The given functions estimate the number of leaves as a function of the t days after April 5th. On which day is it estimated that the trees will have the same number of leaves?

A) April 9th

B) April 10th

C) April 11th

D) April 12th

11.

$$3y + x = 2$$
$$9y + x = 14$$

If (x, y) is the solution to the system of equations above, what is the value of y?

12.

$$E(t) = 1252 + 12t$$
$$W(t) = 1436 - 34t$$

A town with two high schools created the functions above to model the number of students predicted to be enrolled at East High, $E(t)$, and West High, $W(t)$, t years from now. In how many years is the number of students enrolled at each school predicted to be the same?

A) 3

B) 4

C) 5

D) 6

13.

$$5x - 3y = 8$$
$$x - 3y = 4$$

The solution to the given system of equations is (x, y). What is the value of x?

14.

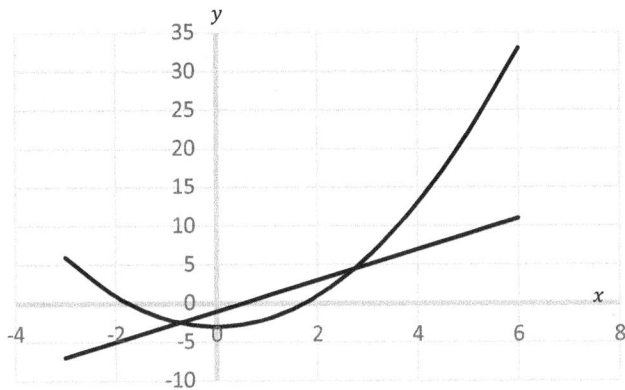

The graph of the system of equations above in the xy-plane consists of a linear equation and a quadratic equation for $-3 \leq x \leq 6$. How many solutions does this system have?

A) 0

B) 1

C) 2

D) 3

15.

$$y = 2x$$
$$5 - 2y = 6x$$

In the xy-plane, what is the y-coordinate of the point of intersection of the graphs with equations above?

A) 1

B) 2

C) 3

D) 4

16.

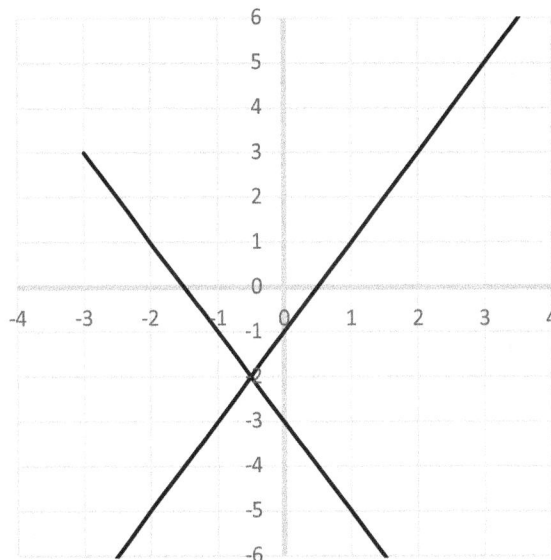

Which of the following systems of equations represents the graph above in the xy-plane?

A) $y + 2x = -1$
   $y - 2x = -3$

B) $y - 2x = -1$
   $y + 2x = -3$

C) $y - 2x = \frac{1}{2}$
   $y + 2x = -\frac{3}{2}$

D) $y + 2x = \frac{1}{2}$
   $y - 2x = -\frac{3}{2}$

17.

If $y = 2x + 3$ and $3x - 4y = 23$, what is the value of x?

A) -4

B) -7

C) -11

D) -14

18.

$$y = 2x - 4$$
$$y = 3x + 1$$

The solution to the system of equations above is (x, y). What is the value of x?

A) -1

B) -3

C) -5

D) -7

19.

At a local high school, there are a total of 1,524 students and teachers. The ratio of students to teachers is 2.2 to 1. Which system of equations represents this situation, in which s is the number of students and t is the number of teachers?

A) $s + t = 1524$
   $2.2s = t$

B) $s + t = 1524$
   $2.2t = s$

C) $s + t = 1524$
   $2.2 = st$

D) $s + t = 1524$
   $2.2 = \dfrac{1}{st}$

20.

$$3x - 2y = 5$$
$$5x + 2y = 11$$

The solution to the system of equations above is (x, y). What is the value of y?

A) $\dfrac{1}{4}$

B) $\dfrac{1}{2}$

C) 1

D) 2

21.

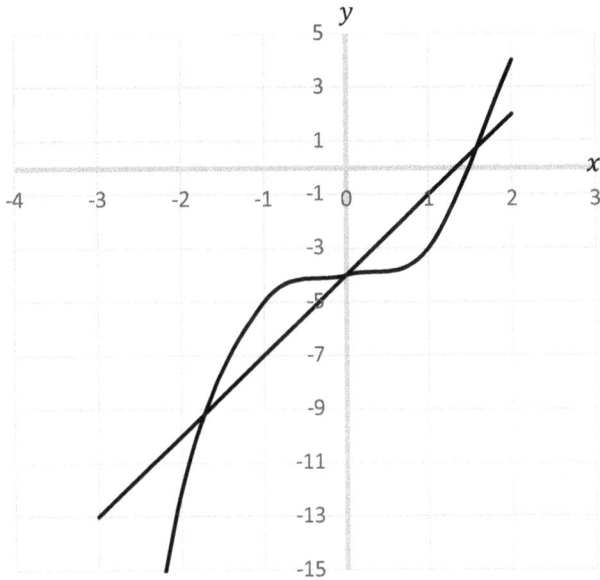

The graph of the system of equations above in the xy-plane consists of a linear equation and a cubic polynomial equation for $-3 \leq x \leq 2$. How many solutions does this system have?

A) 0

B) 1

C) 2

D) 3

22.

Fun Land charges $6 for an adult ticket and $2 for a children's ticket. If Fun Land collects $204 from selling 62 tickets, which of the following systems of equations could be used to determine how many adult tickets, a, and how many children's tickets, c, were sold?

A) $a + c = 204$
$6a + 2c = 62$

B) $6c + 2a = 204$
$a + c = 62$

C) $6a = 2c + 204$
$a + c = 62$

D) $6a + 2c = 204$
$a + c = 62$

23.

A hardwood floor installer purchased a shipment of wood for $360.00. It consisted of P feet of pine floorboards and W feet of walnut floorboards. The cost per foot of the pine floorboards was $2.00 and the cost per foot of the walnut floorboards was $3.50. If the floor installer purchased 120 feet of floorboards in total, how many feet of walnut floorboards did he purchase?

A) 20

B) 40

C) 80

D) 120

24.

$$3y + 4x = 8$$
$$9y + 20x = 12$$

If the solution to the system of equations above is (x, y), what is the value of $|x|$?

25.

$$5x - 6y = 12$$
$$4x - 2y = -6$$

The solution to the given system of equations is (x, y). What is the value of $x - 4y$?

A) 0

B) 6

C) 12

D) 18

26.

$$3(x - y) = 35$$
$$x + 3y = 15$$

The solution to the given system of equations is (x, y). What is the value of $4x$?

27.

$$-2x + 3y = 7$$
$$-3x + 4y = 6$$

The solution to the given system of equations is (x, y). What is the value of $x - y$?

A) 0

B) 1

C) 2

D) 3

28.

$$-4x + 6y = 2$$
$$-2x - 2y = -8$$

The solution to the given system of equations is (x, y). What is the value of $8y - 2x$?

29.

$$2x - 3y = -11$$
$$3x + 2y = 16$$

If the solution to the system of equations above is (x, y), what is the value of x?

30.

In the xy-plane, the graph of $y = -\frac{1}{2}x + 2$ intersects the graph of $y = \frac{5}{2}x - 1$ at the point with coordinates (c, d). What is the value of d?

A) $\frac{1}{2}$

B) 1

C) $\frac{3}{2}$

D) 2

31.

$$6x + 2y = 11$$
$$3x - 8y = 1$$

The solution to the given system of equations is (x, y). What is the value of y?

32.

$$2x + 4y = 13$$
$$4x + 2y = -1$$

The solution to the given system of equations is (x, y). What is the value of $3x + 3y$?

33.

$$y = 2x + 5$$
$$y = 3x^2$$

The graph of the system of equations has an intersection point (x, y) in which $x > 0$ and $y > 0$. What is the x-coordinate of that intersection point?

A) -1

B) 0

C) 1

D) $\frac{5}{3}$

34.

$$3x - 5y = 12$$
$$2x + 2y = -5$$

If (x, y) Is a solution to the system of equations above, what is the value of $50x - 30y$?

35.

A cafeteria sells hot lunches for $5 and cold lunches for $4. If the cafeteria collects $176 one day by selling 40 lunches, how many hot lunches did the cafeteria sell?

36.

$$x + 5y = 6$$
$$3(x + 5y) = 18$$

How many solutions does the given system of equations have?

A) Zero

B) Exactly one

C) Exactly two

D) Infinitely many

37.

The number y is 6 less than twice x. The number y is also 20% less than x. What is the value of y?

A) 3

B) 4

C) 5

D) 6

38.

$$x + 2y = -1$$
$$x - 2y = x^2 - 2$$

If (x, y) Is a solution to the system of equations above, what is a possible value of y?

A) 0

B) 2

C) 4

D) 6

39.

$$3x + 4y = 2$$
$$-2x + 2y = -4$$

The solution to the given system of equations is (x, y). What is the value of x?

40.

$$5x + 3y = 25$$
$$4x + 7y = -3$$

The solution to the given system of equations is (x, y). What is the value of x?

41.

The quadratic function f is defined by $f(x) = ax^2 + b$, where a and b are constants. If $f(2) = 4$ and $f(3) = 6$, what is the value of b?

42.

$$-6x + y = -15$$
$$1.5x - 0.25y = n$$

In the system of equations above, n is a constant. If the system has infinitely many solutions, what is the value of n?

43.

$$x - 5y = 3$$
$$kx + 4y = 4$$

In the system of equations above, k is a constant. For what value of k will the system have no solution?

A) $-\frac{5}{4}$

B) $-\frac{4}{5}$

C) 3

D) 4

44.

$$2x - 3y = 10$$
$$y = px - 2$$

In the system of equations above, p is a constant. For what value of p will the system have no solution?

A) $\frac{2}{3}$

B) $\frac{3}{2}$

C) 2

D) 3

45.

$$x - 4y = -12$$
$$ax + \frac{1}{2}y = b$$

In the system of equations above, a and b are constants. If the system has infinitely many solutions, what is the value of b?

46.

$$qx + 2y = 2$$
$$6x + 4y = 0$$

In the system of equations above, q is a constant. For what value of q will this system of equations have no solution?

A) -6

B) 0

C) 3

D) 6

47.

$$y = 3x - 4$$
$$y = kx - 2$$

In the given system of equations, k is a constant. The system has exactly one solution. Which of the following could be the value of k?

    I.   3
    II. −4
    III. −2

A) I, II, and III

B) II and III only

C) III only

D) None of the above

48.

$$3x + \frac{1}{2}y = 4$$
$$ax + 2y = 4b$$

In the given system of equations, a and b are constants. The system has infinitely many solutions. What is the value of $a + b$?

A) 4

B) 8

C) 12

D) 16

49.

In the lunchroom students are seated at large tables. If there are 12 students per table, 2 tables are not used. If there are 8 students per table, 1 additional table will be needed to seat all the students. How many tables are there currently in the lunchroom?

A) 6

B) 8

C) 10

D) 12

50.

$$\frac{3}{4}x + \frac{1}{2}y = \frac{1}{8}$$
$$ax - 2y = 2b$$

In the system of equations above, a and b are constants. If the system of equations has an infinite number of solutions (x, y), what is the value of b?

A) $-\frac{1}{2}$

B) $-\frac{1}{4}$

C) 0

D) $\frac{1}{4}$

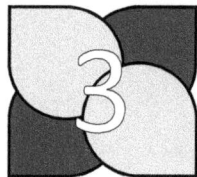

Quadratic Equations

1.

Which of the following is equivalent to $(x - 3)(x + 4)$?

A) $x^2 - 7x - 12$

B) $x^2 - x - 12$

C) $x^2 - x + 12$

D) $x^2 + x - 12$

2.

What is the product of xy^3 and x^2y?

A) x^2y^3

B) x^3y^4

C) x^2y^5

D) x^3y^5

3.

Which of the following expressions is equivalent to $x^2 - (x - 3)$?

A) $x^2 - x - 3$

B) $x^2 + x + 3$

C) $x^2 - x + 3$

D) $x^2 + x - 3$

4.

$$(3x^3 - 4x^2) - (2x^3 - 2x^2)$$

Which of the following expressions is equivalent to the expression given above?

A) $x^3 - 6x^2$

B) $x^3 - 2x^2$

C) $5x^3 - 6x^2$

D) $5x^3 - 2x^2$

5.

Which of the following is equivalent to the expression $(x - 2)^2 + 3$?

A) $x^2 - 1$

B) $x^2 + 7$

C) $x^2 - 4x - 1$

D) $x^2 - 4x + 7$

6.

$$2x^2(x^3 + 2x)$$

The expression above is equivalent to $2x^a + bx^c$, in which a, b, and c are constants. What is the value of abc?

7.

$$x^2 - 6x + 9 = 0$$

What value of x is a solution to the given equation?

A) -3

B) 3

C) 6

D) 9

8.

$$f(x) = -2(x + 2)(x - 3)(x - 1)$$

In the xy-plane, for how many of the x-intercepts, (x, y), of the graph of the function above is $x \geq 0$?

A) Zero

B) One

C) Two

D) Three

9.

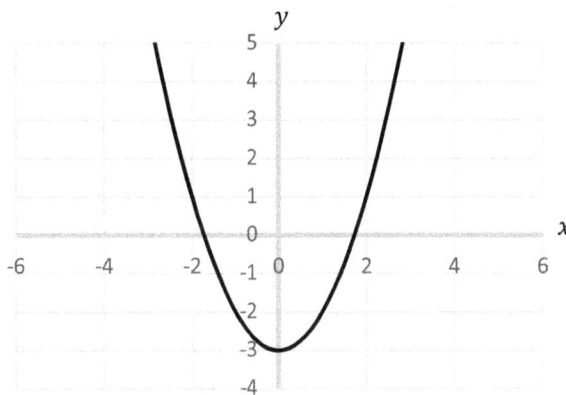

The graph of $y = f(x)$ is shown in the xy-plane above. Which of the following could be the equation of f?

A) $f(x) = -x^2 + 3$

B) $f(x) = -x^2 - 3$

C) $f(x) = x^2 - 3$

D) $f(x) = -3x^2$

10.

$$(4x - 5)(3x + 4) = 0$$

Which of the following is a solution to the equation above?

A) $-\dfrac{5}{4}$

B) $-\dfrac{3}{4}$

C) $\dfrac{5}{4}$

D) $\dfrac{4}{3}$

11.

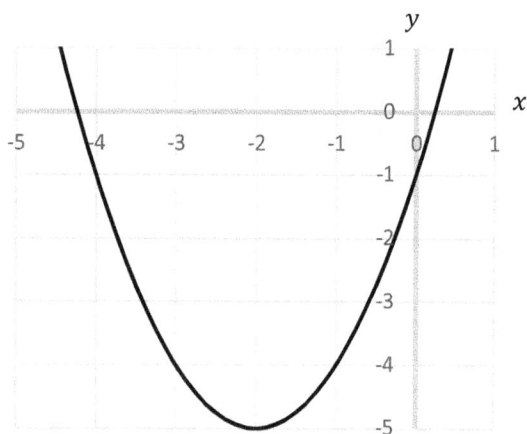

Which of the following is an equation of the graph above in the xy-plane?

A) $y = -(x + 2)^2 - 5$

B) $y = -(x - 2)^2 - 5$

C) $y = (x + 2)^2 - 5$

D) $y = (x - 2)^2 - 5$

12.

$$9\left(\frac{x}{3} + 1\right)^2$$

Which of the following is equivalent to the expression above?

A) $x^2 + 9$

B) $3x^2 + 9$

C) $x^2 + 3x + 9$

D) $x^2 + 6x + 9$

13.

If $2(2x - 1)(x + 3) = ax^2 + bx + c$, what is the value of ab?

14.

$$(5x - 2)(4x + 1) = ax^2 + bx + c$$

In the equation above, $a, b,$ and c are constants. If the equation is true for all values of x, what is the value of $a + b + c$?

15.

$$x^2(x-2) - 4(x-2) = 0$$

In the equation above, $x \geq 0$. What is the value of x?

A) 0

B) 2

C) 4

D) 6

16.

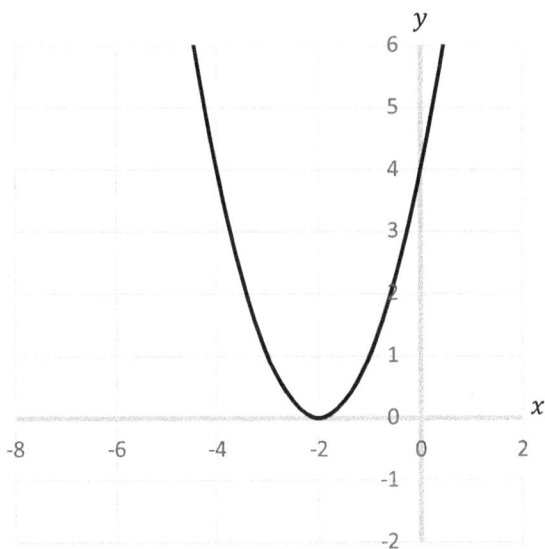

Which of the following is the equation of the graph above, in the xy-plane?

A) $y = x^2 + 4$

B) $y = (x-2)^2$

C) $y = (x+2)^2$

D) $y = (x+2)^2 + 4$

17.

$$x^2 + 3x - 11 = 0$$

If a solution to the equation above can be written as $\dfrac{-3 \pm \sqrt{n}}{2}$, where n is a constant, what is the value of n?

18.

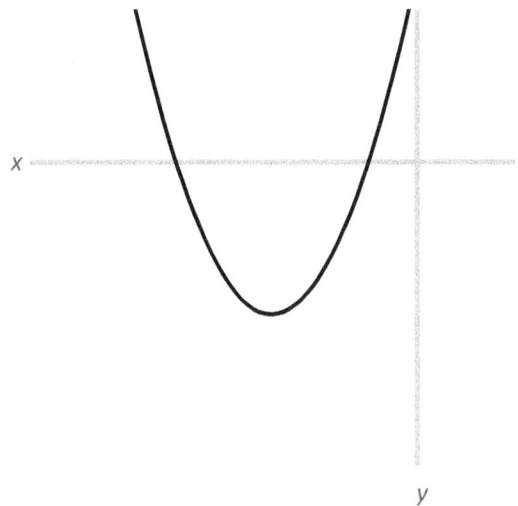

Which of the following could be the equation of the graph above?

A) $y = (x-1)(x-3)$

B) $y = (x+1)(x-3)$

C) $y = (x-1)(x+3)$

D) $y = (x+1)(x+3)$

19.

$$(x^4 - 1)(x + 2) = 0$$

How many real solutions does the equation above have?

A) One

B) Two

C) Three

D) Four

20.

Which of the following is a factor of the expression $(x^2 - 3x)(x^2 - 4)$?

    I. $x - 3$
    II. $x + 2$
    III. $x - 2$

A) I only

B) I and III

C) II and III

D) I, II, and III

21.

$$x(x - 1)(x + 2) = ax^3 + bx^2 + cx$$

In the equation above, a, b, and c are constants. If the equation is true for all values of x, what is the value of $a + b + c$?

A) 0

B) 2

C) 4

D) 6

22.

$$c = x^2 + 3x - 4$$
$$d = x + 2$$

Which of the following expressions is equivalent to cd?

A) $x^3 + 3x^2 + 6x - 8$

B) $x^3 + 5x^2 + 2x - 8$

C) $x^3 + 3x^2 - 10x - 8$

D) $x^3 + 5x^2 + 6x - 8$

23.

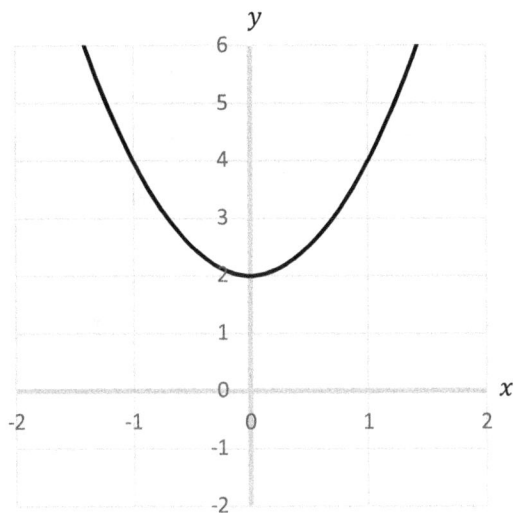

Which equation represents the graph above in the xy-plane?

A) $y = \frac{1}{2}x^2 + 2$

B) $y = x^2 + 2$

C) $y = 2x^2 + 2$

D) $y = 3x^2 + 2$

24.

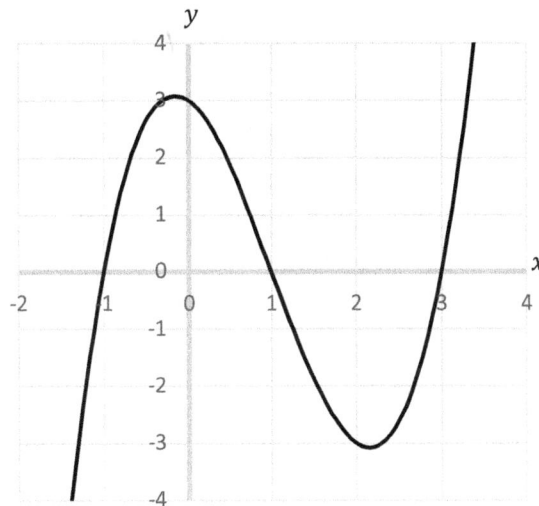

The graph above is defined by $f(x) = (x + a)(x + b)(x + c)$, where a, b, and c are constants. What is the value of $a + b + c$?

A) -5

B) -3

C) -2

D) 3

25.

$$(x + 3) = (x - 2)(x + 3)$$

What is the positive solution to the equation above?

26.

If $x^2 - 2x + 1 = 0$, what is the value of $x + 3$?

A) 1

B) 2

C) 3

D) 4

27.

$$x^2 + 7x + 6 = 0$$

If the solutions to the equation above are $\dfrac{-7 \pm \sqrt{a}}{2}$, where a is a constant, what is the value of a?

28.

$$x(x - 2)(x + 3)(x - a) = 0$$

In the equation above, a is a constant. The sum of the solutions to the equation is 3. What is the value of a?

29.

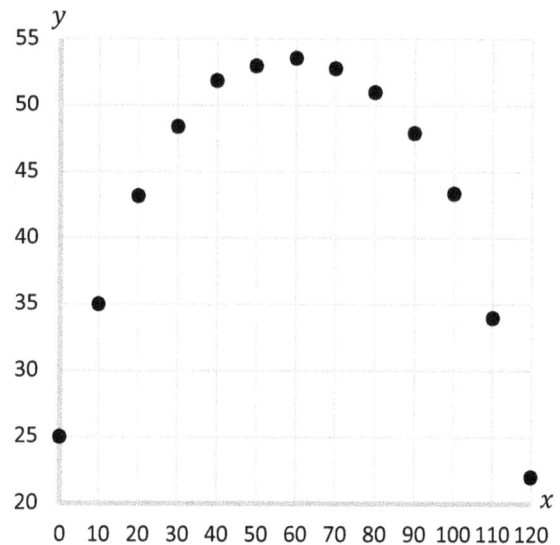

Which of the following quadratic equations best models the data in the scatterplot above?

A) $y = 0.008x^2 + x + 25$

B) $y = 0.008x^2 - x + 25$

C) $y = -0.008x^2 + x + 25$

D) $y = -0.008x^2 - x + 25$

30.

The solutions to the equation $x^2 - 3x = 2$ can be written as $\dfrac{a \pm \sqrt{b}}{2}$, where a and b are constants. What is the value of $a + b$?

31.

Which of the following is a solution to the equation $x^2 + 3x = 1$?

A) $\dfrac{-3+\sqrt{13}}{2}$

B) $\dfrac{3-\sqrt{13}}{2}$

C) $\dfrac{-3+\sqrt{5}}{2}$

D) $\dfrac{3-\sqrt{5}}{2}$

32.

$$\frac{x^4 - 81}{x - 3}$$

If $x \neq 3$, which of the following is equivalent to the expression above?

A) $x^3 + 27$

B) $x^3 - 27$

C) $(x^2 + 9)(x + 3)$

D) $(x + 3)(x + 3)$

33.

If there is only one real value of x that satisfies the equation $4x^2 - 5x + c = 0$, what is the value of c?

A) $\dfrac{25}{2}$

B) $\dfrac{25}{4}$

C) $\dfrac{25}{16}$

D) $\dfrac{5}{4}$

34.

If $x^2 - 2x - 5 = 0$, which of the following is a possible value of $x - 1$?

A) $\sqrt{6}$

B) $\sqrt{18}$

C) $\sqrt{22}$

D) $\sqrt{24}$

35.

Which of the following represents the solutions to the equation $x(x - 6) = -6$?

A) $3 \pm \sqrt{60}$

B) $3 \pm \sqrt{15}$

C) $3 \pm \sqrt{12}$

D) $3 \pm \sqrt{3}$

36.

$$9x^2 + 24x + c = 0$$

In the equation above, c is a constant. If the graph of the equation contains two distinct x-intercepts, which of the following CANNOT be the value of c?

A) 4

B) 8

C) 12

D) 16

37.

$$f(x) = 3x^2 - 4x + 2$$

For what value of x does $f(x)$ reach its minimum value?

38.

$$(x + 2)(x - 1)(x^2 - 4x + 6) = 0$$

How many real solutions does the equation above have?

A) One

B) Two

C) Three

D) Four

39.

$$4x^2 + bx + 25 = 0$$

In the equation above, b is a positive constant. If the equation has exactly one solution, what is the value of b?

A) 5

B) 10

C) 20

D) 100

40.

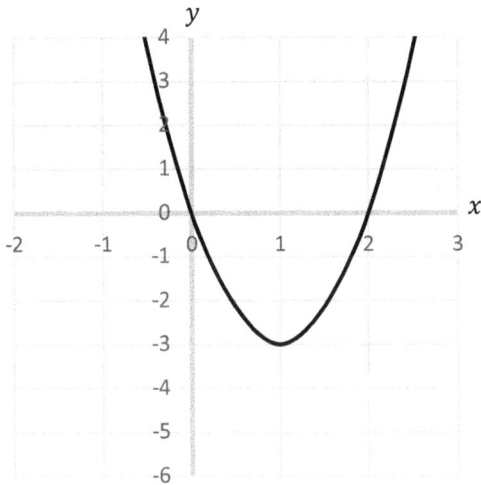

Which of the following is an equation of the parabola graphed above in the xy-plane?

A) $y = 3x(x - 2)$

B) $y = 3x(x + 2)$

C) $y = 3x(x - 1)$

D) $y = 3x(x + 1)$

41.

What is the larger of the two solutions to the quadratic equation $3x(x + 2) = 6x(x - 1)$?

42.

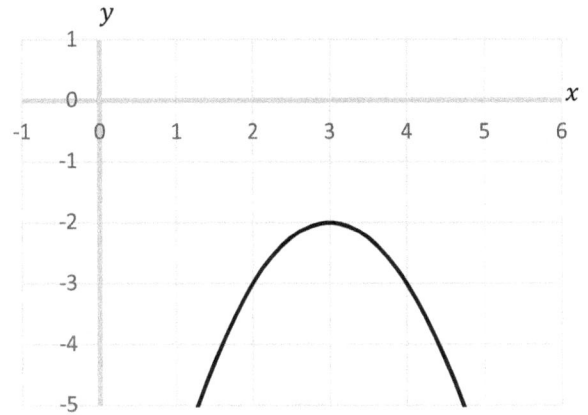

The figure above shows the graph of the function $y = f(x)$. The function g (not shown) is defined by the equation $g(x) = -(x - 1)^2 + 2$. How much greater is the maximum value of $g(x)$ than the maximum value of $f(x)$?

A) 1

B) 2

C) 3

D) 4

43.

$$2x^2 - 5x - 42 = 0$$

What is the positive solution to the given equation?

44.

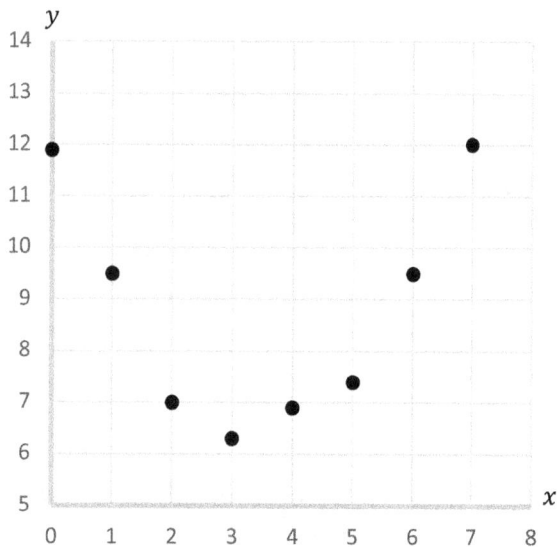

Which of the following quadratic equations best models the data in the scatterplot above?

A) $y = 0.7x^2 - 4.4x + 12.8$

B) $y = 0.7x^2 + 4.4x + 12.8$

C) $y = 0.7x^2 - 4.4x - 12.8$

D) $y = 0.7x^2 + 4.4x - 12.8$

45.

$$(x + 2)^2 - (2 - x)^2$$

The expression above is equivalent to $ax^2 + bx + c$, in which $a, b,$ and c are constants. What is the value of b?

46.

$$x^2 + bx + 3 = 0$$

In the equation above, b is a constant. If the equation has no real solutions, which of the following could be the value of b?

A) 3

B) 4

C) 5

D) 6

47.

Which one of the following equations has a minimum value of a, where a is a positive constant?

A) $y = ax^2$

B) $y = (x - a)^2$

C) $y = a(x + 2)^2$

D) $y = x^2 + a$

48.

$$6x^3 + 6x^2 - 12x$$

The expression above can be rewritten as $ax(x + 2)(x - b)$, where a and b are constants. What is the value of b?

49.

$$h(t) = -2t^2 + 12t + 4$$

The function above models the height, h, in feet, above the ground t seconds after a ball is thrown straight upward into the air. Which of the following represents the maximum height, in feet, that the ball is thrown?

A) 3

B) 4

C) 12

D) 22

50.

$$x^2 - 2x + c = 0$$

In the equation above, c is a constant. If $\sqrt{4 - 4c} = 6$ and $x > 0$, what is the value of x?

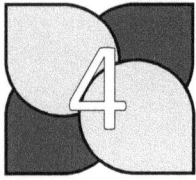

Percents

1.

City	Total Population (18+)	Total Population (All)
Bloomfield	34,315	44,110
Springfield	11,231	16,420
Washington	24,255	31,100
Riverton	8,923	12,155
Salem	13,139	17,198

The table gives the total adult population and the total population, including those under 18 years of age, for five local towns. Bloomfield's total adult population (18+) is p percent of its total population. What is the value of p, rounded to the nearest whole number?

2.

What is 5% of 55?

A) 2.75

B) 5.5

C) 11

D) 27.5

3.

A human resources manager interviewed 40 applicants for a job opening. 60% had the necessary experience for the job. How many of the job applicants had the necessary experience?

4.

A trail mix contains 15% peanuts, by weight. How much of a 16-ounce bag of trail mix, in ounces, is peanuts?

A) 1.5

B) 2.0

C) 2.4

D) 3.0

5.

At a company, 1022 employees responded to whether he or she will attend the annual holiday party. The results are below:

Response	# of Responses
Yes	322
No	613
Maybe	87

If $p\%$ of the respondents said "maybe," what is the value of p, to the nearest tenth?

6.

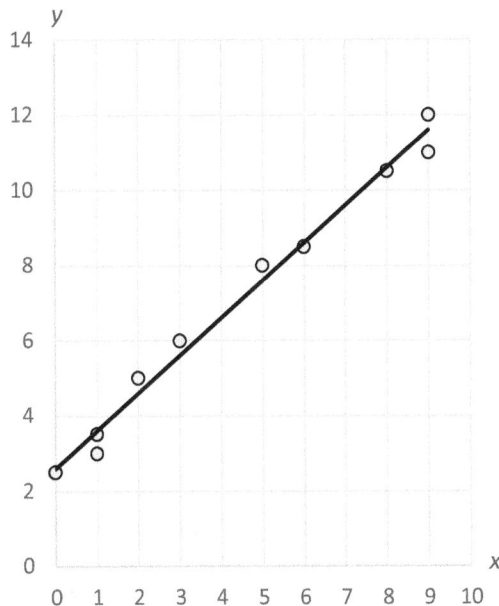

In the scatterplot above, p percent of the 10 data points are greater than the value predicted by the line of best fit. What is the value of p?

7.

What number is 10% less than 8000?

8.

What percentage of 30 is 6?

A) 2%

B) 6%

C) 20%

D) 500%

9.

Grade	Number of students
9th	422
10th	356
11th	443
12th	402

A local high school consists of grades 9 through 12. Students in 9th grade are p percent of the total number of students in the high school. What is the value of p, to the nearest whole number?

10.

A car dealership has 122 cars in stock. If 14 new cars get delivered to the car dealership, what is the percent increase in the number of cars at the dealership?

A) 8.7%

B) 10.3%

C) 11.5%

D) 12.2%

11.

If $x\%$ of 72 is 9, what is the value of x?

A) 12.5

B) 15

C) 17.5

D) 20

12.

A banner for the school play is 12 feet long. A larger version of the banner is needed for the outside of the school that is 75% longer than the original banner. How long, in feet, will the new banner be?

A) 20

B) 21

C) 22

D) 23

13.

What is the result when 160 is increased by 30 percent?

14.

Score Range	Class 1	Class 2	Class 3
60-69	6	4	2
70-79	14	12	10
80-89	2	4	10
90-100	2	2	3
Total	24	22	25

In June, all students in the three 12th grade classes at Mountain High School took the final exam. A table with the results is above. Approximately what percent of all the final scores in classes 2 and 3 were in the 80-89 range?

A) 18%

B) 22%

C) 30%

D) 40%

15.

Sarah's brother, on average, consumes 30% more calories per day than Sarah. If her brother consumes, on average, 1690 calories per day, how many calories does Sarah consume, on average, per day?

16.

	White	Brown	Black	Green	Blue	Red
House	30	5	1	3	10	8
Apartment	0	2	0	0	0	1
School	1	1	0	0	0	1

Sheila created a table to show the distribution of the colors of her town's houses, apartment buildings, and schools. If 30% of the white houses in the town are in Sheila's neighborhood, how many white houses are in Sheila's neighborhood?

A) 3

B) 6

C) 9

D) 12

17.

The school auditorium can hold 250 students. Plans for a new school include an auditorium that can hold 40% more students. How many students will the new auditorium hold?

A) 100

B) 300

C) 350

D) 400

18.

Sam gets an additional 20% employee discount off the final price of any item for working at a local department store. If Sam buys a television during a 25% off sale that cost $200 prior to the sale, how much would Sam pay after the sale and employee discount?

A) $110

B) $120

C) $135

D) $160

19.

What is the result when 220 is increased by 35 percent?

20.

A tree that is 55 feet tall was 35 feet tall 10 years ago. What is the percent increase in the height of the tree over these 10 years?

A) 18.2%

B) 28.6%

C) 36.4%

D) 57.1%

21.

A home improvement store gives veterans a 10% discount on all purchases. If a veteran pays $22.00 for an item after the discount is applied, what was the price of the item before the discount?

A) $24.20

B) $24.44

C) $25.00

D) $220.00

22.

A food truck was listed for sale for $22,500. After the seller could not find a buyer, he decreased the price to $18,000. What was the percent decrease of the price of the food truck?

23.

A runner averages 11.9 seconds in the 100-meter dash. His goal for this year is to decrease that average time by 15%. At the end of the year, what should his time be in the 100-meter dash, rounded to the nearest tenth of a second?

24.

In April, a gardener planted a t inch tomato plant in his garden. He predicts that the tomato plant will grow to 150% of its current height by May. In terms of t, which of the following represents the gardener's predicted height, in inches, of the tomato plant?

A) $0.5t$

B) $1.5t$

C) $2.5t$

D) $15t$

25.

Month	Snowfall (inches)
January	8
February	20
March	24
April	4

The table above shows the snowfall amounts for a town in the first 4 months of 2021. If the average snowfall per month over the first four months in 2021 is 40% higher than it was in 2020, what was the average snowfall per month, in inches, over the first four months of 2020?

A) 8.4

B) 10.0

C) 12.4

D) 19.6

26.

There were approximately 3,100 baristas in a large city in 2017. The city government predicts that this number will increase to approximately 4,250 from 2017 to 2027. Which of the following is the closest to the percentage increase in the number of baristas in the city from 2017 to 2027?

A) 27%

B) 37%

C) 52%

D) 73%

27.

The expression px, in which p is a constant, represents decreasing the positive number x by 25%. What is the value of p?

28.

A teacher needs to buy paper for her classroom. Each ream of paper costs $7 and tax is an additional 7% of the total cost. If she has $100 to spend on paper, what is the maximum number of reams of paper that the teacher can buy?

29.

A sample of residents of a town was selected at random. The percent of residents in the sample that were 65 years of age or older was 43%, with a margin of error of 7%. If there are 5,500 residents of the town, which of the following could be the number of residents 65 years of age or older?

A) 1970

B) 2475

C) 2765

D) 2790

30.

Which of the following represents the value of n decreased by 7%?

A) $0.3n$

B) $0.7n$

C) $0.93n$

D) $-7n$

31.

A machine that fills cereal boxes normally fills 75% of the volume of the box with cereal. A broken dispenser has caused the machine to only fill 90% of its normal amount. What percentage, rounded to the nearest whole number, of the volume of the box will be filled by the machine with the broken dispenser?

A) 60%

B) 68%

C) 75%

D) 83%

32.

A drink mix requires s scoops of powder mix for every 2 quarts of water. Mason accidently used 25% less drink mix than required. How many scoops did Mason use in terms of s?

A) .25s

B) .75s

C) 1.25s

D) 25s

33.

A small town grew from 138 residents in 2010 to 213 residents in 2020. The population in 2020 was p% greater than the population in 2010. What is the value of p, rounded to the nearest whole number?

34.

In 1930, The Chrysler Building was the tallest building in New York City, with a total height of 1,046 feet. Upon completion the following year, the Empire State Building, 1.2 times the height of the Chrysler Building, became the tallest building in New York City. The height of the Empire State Building is what percent greater than the height of the Chrysler Building?

A) 2%

B) 12%

C) 20%

D) 120%

35.

In 2005, there were 9 students for every teacher at a local elementary school. In 2020, there were 7.2 students for every teacher at that elementary school. What is the percent decrease in the number of students per teacher from 2005 to 2020, rounded to the nearest tenth?

A) 11.1

B) 13.9

C) 20.0

D) 25.0

36.

Charles invested $25,000 into a mutual fund. Two years later, the investment had grown by 2.23%. The value of his investment is now how many times his initial investment?

A) 1.00223

B) 1.0223

C) 1.223

D) 2.23

37.

Approximately 65% of a homeowner's loan has been paid off. If L is the amount, in dollars, of the original loan, and R is the amount, in dollars, remaining to be paid off, which of the following equations represents R, in terms of L?

A) $R = 65L$

B) $R = .35L$

C) $R = .65L$

D) $R = .35L + .65$

38.

A neighborhood drainage pond initially covered d square yards. After a large rainstorm, the pond grew to 225% of its original area. Which of the following expressions represents the area of the drainage pond after the rainstorm?

A) $0.225d$

B) $2.25d$

C) $22.5d$

D) $225d$

39.

The number of hurricanes decreased by 20% from 2017 to 2018. If there were h hurricanes in 2017, which expression represents the number of hurricanes in 2018, in terms of h?

A) $120h$

B) $80h$

C) $0.8h$

D) $0.2h$

40.

The number of travelers arriving at an airport decreased by 34.2% from February to March. The airport saw 12,365 travelers arrive in March. Approximately how many travelers arrived at the airport in February?

A) 4,230

B) 16,590

C) 18,790

D) 36,160

41.

A carpenter builds a table that is 12 feet long by 4 feet wide. He wants to build a new table with the same ratio of length to width, but an area that is 25% larger. What will be the length of the newly built table?

A) 5

B) $2\sqrt{5}$

C) $6\sqrt{5}$

D) 15

42.

The positive number a is 35% greater than the positive number b. Which of the following represents b, in terms of a?

A) $\dfrac{a}{.35}$

B) $\dfrac{a}{.65}$

C) $\dfrac{a}{1.35}$

D) $\dfrac{a}{1.65}$

43.

Which of the following expressions represents the positive number n increased by 15%?

A) $0.15n$

B) $0.85n$

C) $1.15n$

D) $1.5n$

44.

Matt is 15 years old, three years older than his sister Paola. Matt's age is p percent greater than the age of his sister. What is the value of p?

A) 20%

B) 25%

C) 30%

D) 33%

45.

A journalist wrote 16 articles last week. This week, she writes 25% more articles than last week. What percentage, rounded to the nearest tenth, of the total articles that she wrote in the last two weeks did she write this week?

46.

At a local restaurant, 60% of the employees are servers and 40% of the employees are cooks. If 30% of the cooks and 20% of the servers will get a raise at the end of the year, what percent of all employees will get a raise at the end of the year?

A) 24

B) 25

C) 26

D) 27

47.

In a local community, 76% of residents 18 and older and 46% of residents under 18 are vaccinated for an infectious disease. If those 18 and older make up 70% of the population, what percent of the entire community is vaccinated for the infectious disease?

A) 55%

B) 61%

C) 67%

D) 70%

48.

The amount of water in a reservoir decreased by 35% after a recent drought. What remains in the reservoir is x million gallons of water. Which expression gives the value of what the reservoir contained before the drought, in terms of x?

A) $\dfrac{x}{.35}$

B) $\dfrac{x}{.65}$

C) $\dfrac{x}{1.35}$

D) $\dfrac{x}{1.65}$

49.

A newborn horse has legs that measure x inches in length. In two years, the length of the horse's legs is predicted to increase by 112%. Multiplying which of the following by the current leg length of x will give the length of the horse's legs in two years?

A) 0.12

B) 1.12

C) 2.12

D) 112

50.

The cost of a flight from New York to London averaged $800 in 2015. The average cost of the flight increased by 115% from 2015 to 2016 and then decreased by 45% from 2016 to 2017. Which of the following expressions represents the average cost of a flight from New York to London, in dollars, in 2017?

A) $(1.15)(1.45)(800)$

B) $(2.15)(1.45)(800)$

C) $(1.15)(0.55)(800)$

D) $(2.15)(0.55)(800)$

Solving

1.

$$x - 3 = 2 - 3x$$

What is the solution to the equation above?

A) $\frac{1}{4}$

B) $\frac{4}{5}$

C) $\frac{5}{4}$

D) $\frac{5}{2}$

2.

If $4y - 7 = 3y + 2$, what is the value of y?

A) -9

B) -5

C) $\frac{9}{7}$

D) 9

3.

$$y = x^2 - 3x + 2$$

In the equation above, what is the value of y when $x = 4$?

A) -6

B) -3

C) 3

D) 6

4.

$$7x - 4 = 24$$

If x is the solution to the equation above, what is the value of $7x$?

A) 4

B) 7

C) 20

D) 28

5.

$$7x + 2 = x - 31$$

What is the solution to the given equation?

A) $-\dfrac{33}{6}$

B) $-\dfrac{29}{6}$

C) $-\dfrac{33}{8}$

D) $-\dfrac{29}{8}$

6.

$$7(x - 2) = 56$$

What is the solution to the given equation?

A) 7

B) 8

C) $\dfrac{58}{7}$

D) 10

7.

If $10x - 20 = 30$, what is the value of $2x - 4$?

A) 5

B) 6

C) 7

D) 8

8.

$$\frac{3}{2}x - 4 = 11$$

What is the solution to the given equation?

9.

$$15x = 3y$$

Which one of the following equations gives x in terms of y?

A) $x = \dfrac{1}{5}y$

B) $x = 5y$

C) $x = 12y$

D) $x = 18y$

10.

$$23 = x + 4 + 4x - 2 - 2x$$

Which of the following is a solution to the equation above?

A) 5

B) 7

C) $\frac{17}{2}$

D) 9

11.

$$\frac{2}{5} = \frac{x - 1}{10}$$

What value of x satisfies the equation?

A) 4

B) $\frac{21}{5}$

C) 5

D) 26

12.

$$\frac{1}{4}x - 2 = 10$$

What value of x satisfies the equation above?

13.

$$2(x + 3) = -2 + 3(x + 3)$$

In the equation above, what is the value of $x + 3$?

A) -1

B) 0

C) 1

D) 2

14.

If $3y = 6y - 1$, what is the value of y?

15.

What is the solution to the equation
$2x + 6 = 3(x - 2)$?

A) 0

B) 4

C) 8

D) 12

16.

If $4x = x + 9$, what is the value of $6x$?

A) 3

B) 6

C) 9

D) 18

17.

$$2(x + 3) = -2(x - 3)$$

In the given equation, what is the value of x?

18.

If $6x + 12 = 2x + 28$, what is the value of x?

A) 0

B) 2

C) 4

D) 6

19.

$$K = \frac{F - 32}{1.8} + 273.15$$

The equation above can be used to convert a temperature F, in degrees Fahrenheit, to a temperature K, in Kelvin. Which of the following, in Kelvin, is closest to a temperature of 51.8°F?

A) 271

B) 275

C) 284

D) 293

20.

If $5x - 4 = 6$, what is the value of $15x - 12$?

21.

If $2x + 1 = 3$, what is the value of $8x + 4$?

A) 1

B) 2

C) 4

D) 12

22.

If $\sqrt{x^2 - 4x + 4} = 8$ and $x \geq 0$, what is the value of x?

23.

$$px + 14 = 3x + 28$$

In the equation above, p is a constant. For what value of p will the equation above have no solution?

A) −3

B) −2

C) 2

D) 3

24.

$$r = \sqrt{\frac{A}{\pi}}$$

The equation above can be used to find the radius, r, of a circle with a given area, A. What is the radius of a circle with an area of 24π?

A) $2\sqrt{6}$

B) $2\sqrt{12}$

C) $4\sqrt{6}$

D) $4\sqrt{12}$

25.

$$|2x - 3| = 7$$

What is the sum of the solutions to the equation above?

26.

$$m + 5n = 2p$$

Which of following equations expresses n in terms of m and p?

A) $n = \dfrac{2p+m}{5}$

B) $n = \dfrac{m-2p}{5}$

C) $n = \dfrac{2m-p}{5}$

D) $n = \dfrac{2p-m}{5}$

27.

$$\sqrt{2x} = 8$$

What are all the values of x that satisfy the equation above?

A) 4 only

B) 32 only

C) -4 and 4

D) -32 and 32

28.

$$\frac{81}{x^3} = -3$$

What is a solution to the given equation?

A) -3

B) $-\dfrac{1}{3}$

C) 3

D) There is no solution for x

29.

$$x = \frac{3}{5}y$$

The equation above shows the relationship between two variables. Which of the following is equivalent to $10x$, in terms of y?

A) $3y$

B) $6y$

C) $10y$

D) $30y$

30.

$$2x^2 + 2 = n(x^2 + 1)$$

In the equation above, n is a constant. If the equation has an infinite number of solutions, what is the value of n?

A) -1

B) 0

C) 1

D) 2

31.

$$\frac{x+2}{2} = \frac{x-1}{5} - 3$$

What is the value of x in the equation above?

A) -14

B) -10

C) -5

D) -2

32.

A furniture maker uses the formula $w = \frac{1}{4}l + 4$ to calculate the width w, in feet, of a table with a length l, in feet. Which of the following expresses the length of the table in terms of its width?

A) $l = 4w - 4$

B) $l = \frac{1}{4}w - 4$

C) $l = 4w - 16$

D) $l = 4w - 1$

33.

$$\sqrt[4]{(x-2)^4} = 2$$

In the equation above, what is the value of x?

A) 4

B) 10

C) 14

D) 18

34.

$$\frac{2}{3}(9 - 6x) = -3$$

What is the solution to the given equation?

35.

If $\frac{3}{4}(x - 2) + 1 = 7$, what is the value of $x - 2$?

A) 6

B) 8

C) 10

D) 12

36.

$$-2|x + 2| = 20$$

If x is a solution to the equation above, how many possible values of x are there?

A) Zero

B) One

C) Two

D) There are infinite possible values of x

37.

What value of b makes the equation

$$\sqrt{1 + \frac{3}{b}} = 4 \text{ true?}$$

38.

$$x = \frac{k}{y}$$

In the equation above, x and y are variables, and k is a constant. Which of the following expressions is equivalent to $\frac{y}{4}$?

A) $\frac{4k}{x}$

B) $\frac{k}{4x}$

C) $\frac{4x}{k}$

D) $\frac{kx}{4}$

39.

$$cx + 4c = 5c$$

In the equation above, c is a constant. What value of x satisfies the equation above?

40.

$$5(x - 2) - x = 4(x - 1) + ax$$

In the equation above, a is a constant. If the equation above has no solution, what is the value of a?

A) 0

B) 1

C) 2

D) 3

41.

$$\sqrt{-x - 1} = x + 3$$

If x is a solution to the equation above, which of the following could be true?

    I. $x = -5$
    II. $x = -2$

A) I only

B) II only

C) I and II

D) Neither I nor II

42.

$$3x + 4 = nx - 7x - 3$$

In the equation above, n is a constant. If the equation has no solution, what is the value of n?

A) 3

B) 4

C) 7

D) 10

43.

$$|x + 2| = 2x - 3$$

What is the sum of the solutions to the equation above?

44.

$$2(x - 3) - 4 = 2x - a$$

In the equation above, a is a constant. If the equation has infinitely many solutions, what is the value of a?

45.

$$\sqrt{-2x} = x + 4$$

What are all possible solutions to the given equation?

A) $x = -2$

B) $x = 0$

C) $x = \frac{1}{2}$

D) $x = -2$ and $x = -8$

46.

$$(p + 2)x = 5x + 2$$

In the given equation, p is a constant. For what value of p will the given equation have no solution?

A) -2

B) 2

C) 3

D) 5

47.

$$kx - 5x + 2 = 2(2x + 1)$$

In the equation above, k is a constant. If the equation has an infinite number of solutions, what is the value of k?

A) 3

B) 5

C) 7

D) 9

48.

$$2x + 5 = ax + 4$$

In the given equation, a is a constant. If the equation has exactly one solution, which of the following CANNOT be the value of a?

A) 0

B) 1

C) 2

D) 3

49.

If $\dfrac{2}{2y} + \dfrac{2}{y} = 3$, where $y \neq 0$, what is the value of $\dfrac{2}{y}$?

A) $\dfrac{1}{2}$

B) 1

C) 2

D) 4

50.

$$|x - 3| = 5x$$

What is the value of the positive solution to the equation above?

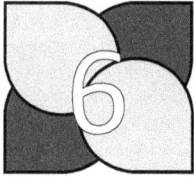

Exponents

1.

$$x^2x^3 = x^n$$

In the equation above, n is a constant. What is the value of n?

A) 1

B) 3

C) 5

D) 6

2.

Which of the following equations is equivalent to $a = b^{\frac{2}{3}}c^{\frac{4}{3}}$?

A) $a = \sqrt[3]{b^2c^4}$

B) $a = \sqrt[4]{b^2c^3}$

C) $a = \sqrt[3]{b^4c^2}$

D) $a = \sqrt[4]{b^6c^3}$

3.

Which expression below is equivalent to the expression $\sqrt{x^2y^4}$, in which x and y are positive constants?

A) $x^{\frac{1}{2}}y^{\frac{1}{4}}$

B) $xy^{\frac{1}{2}}$

C) xy^2

D) xy^4

4.

Which expression is equivalent to $m^2(m^{\frac{3}{2}}n^2p^3)$?

A) $m^3n^2p^3$

B) $m^{\frac{7}{2}}n^2p^3$

C) $m^3n^4p^6$

D) $m^{\frac{7}{2}}n^4p^5$

5.

Which expression is equivalent to $\dfrac{2}{x^{-3}}$?

A) $x^{\frac{2}{3}}$

B) $x^{\frac{3}{2}}$

C) $\dfrac{x^3}{2}$

D) $2x^3$

6.

Which expression below is equivalent to decreasing a positive quantity x by 3.9%?

A) $0.039x$

B) $0.390x$

C) $0.610x$

D) $0.961x$

7.

$$3\sqrt{81x^3}$$

If $x > 0$, which of the following is equivalent to the expression above?

A) $27x^6$

B) $27x^3$

C) $27x^{\frac{2}{3}}$

D) $27x^{\frac{3}{2}}$

8.

The amount of water in a reservoir increases by 12% after a rainstorm. The resulting amount of water is x. Which expression below gives the original amount of water in a reservoir, in terms of x?

A) $0.88x$

B) $1.12x$

C) $\dfrac{x}{.88}$

D) $\dfrac{x}{1.12}$

9.

Which of the following is equivalent to $\sqrt{9x^6}$?

A) $3x^3$

B) $3x^4$

C) $9x^3$

D) $9x^4$

10.

$$A(t) = 1000(1.025)^t$$

The given function shows the amount of money that Joann will have after depositing $1000 into a savings account for t years. According to the function, what is the percent interest that the account accrues each year?

A) 1.025%

B) 2.5%

C) 25%

D) 102.5%

11.

$$(x^3y^4)^{\frac{5}{8}}$$

Which expression is equivalent to the expression above, in which $x > 0$ and $y > 0$?

A) $\sqrt[8]{x^8y^9}$

B) $xy \cdot \sqrt[8]{y}$

C) $xy^2 \cdot \sqrt[8]{x^7y^4}$

D) $x^3y^4 \cdot \sqrt[8]{x^5y^5}$

12.

A small town has lost 3% of its population, on average, per year since 1990. Which of the following types of functions best models the population of the town as a function of the years since 1990?

A) Increasing exponential

B) Decreasing exponential

C) Increasing linear

D) Decreasing linear

13.

A newborn baby is expected to gain 9 pounds per year for the first 3 years of its life. Which of the following types of functions best models the weight of the baby over this time period?

A) Increasing exponential

B) Decreasing exponential

C) Increasing linear

D) Decreasing linear

14.

Which of the following expressions is equivalent to $8(4)^{2x}$?

A) 2^{12x}

B) 2^{4x+3}

C) 4^{3x}

D) 4^{4x}

15.

The expression $2\sqrt{32}$ can be rewritten as $a\sqrt{b}$, in which a and b are integers and $a > b$. What is the value of ab?

A) 16

B) 24

C) 32

D) 64

16.

$$a(t) = 61(1.15)^t$$

The function above models the number of air travelers, $a(t)$, in thousands, at a local airport for the two weeks leading up to Thanksgiving in 2019, where t is the number of days after November 14th. Which of the following is best interpretation of the number 1.15 in this context?

A) There were 1.15 thousand air travelers on November 14th.

B) There was an increase of 1.15 thousand air travelers each day after November 14th.

C) It would take 1.15 days to reach $a(t)$ air travelers.

D) The ratio of air travelers on a day after November 14th to the previous day is 1.15.

17.

$$(\sqrt[3]{x^2})^6 = x^a$$

In the equation above, a is a constant. What is a value of a?

18.

The function $B(t) = 26(3)^{\frac{t}{8}}$ models the number of juniper berries on a tree, in which $B(t)$ is the number of juniper berries and t is the time, in days. What is the best interpretation of the number 26 in this context?

A) The number of juniper berries has tripled 26 times.

B) The number of juniper berries triples every 26 days.

C) The number of juniper berries increased by 26 every eight days.

D) The number of juniper berries on the tree when measurements first began was 26.

19.

A local bakery has increased sales by 4% each month since it first opened. Which type of function would best model this increase in sales?

A) Increasing exponential

B) Decreasing exponential

C) Increasing linear

D) Decreasing linear

20.

Each month, the number of subscribers to a website increases by 6% compared to the previous month. Initially, the website had 1200 subscribers. Which equation gives the number of subscribers, n, after m months?

A) $n = 1200(0.06)^m$

B) $n = 1200(0.6)^m$

C) $n = 1200(1.06)^m$

D) $n = 1200(1.6)^m$

21.

Which of the following is equivalent to $\sqrt[3]{(x-1)^6}$?

A) $(x-1)^{\frac{1}{2}}$

B) $(x-1)$

C) $(x-1)^2$

D) $(x-1)^3$

22.

$$A(t) = 25(0.5)^{\frac{t}{2}}$$

The function above represents the mass, in milligrams, of a certain pharmaceutical remaining in a patient after t hours. Which of the following is the best interpretation of the number 25 in this context?

A) The initial mass, in milligrams, of the pharmaceutical in the patient.

B) The mass, in milligrams, of the pharmaceutical in the patient after 2 hours.

C) The number of hours it takes for half of the pharmaceutical to remain in the patient.

D) The number of hours it takes for 2 milligrams of the pharmaceutical to remain in the patient.

23.

Which expression is equivalent to $xy^{\frac{3}{4}}$, where x and y are positive constants?

A) $x\sqrt[4]{y^3}$

B) $x\sqrt[3]{y^4}$

C) $\sqrt[4]{(xy)^3}$

D) $\sqrt[3]{(xy)^4}$

24.

Which expression below is equivalent to $c^2 d^5 (cd)^3$?

A) $c^3 d^8$

B) $c^5 d^8$

C) $c^2 d^{15}$

D) $c^6 d^{15}$

25.

A runner has a goal to increase his total distance run each day by half a mile over a thirty-day period. On the first day, he runs a total distance of one mile. Which of the following types of equations would best model how the total distance run each day changes over this thirty-day period?

A) Increasing linear

B) Decreasing linear

C) Increasing exponential

D) Decreasing exponential

26.

$$\sqrt{9x^2} + \sqrt[3]{8x^3}$$

If the expression above is equivalent to bx, in which b is a constant, what is the value of b?

27.

$$V(t) = 10(1.8)^t$$

The function above models the velocity of a car over a time period, where $V(t)$ is the velocity and t is the time, in seconds. Which of the following models the velocity of the car after m minutes?

A) $V(m) = 10(1.8)^m$

B) $V(m) = 10(1.8)^{60m}$

C) $V(m) = 10(1.8)^{\frac{m}{60}}$

D) $V(m) = 10(1.8)^{\frac{60}{m}}$

28.

A smartphone's battery has an initial capacity of 2675 milliampere-hours. The battery's capacity decreases by 2% for every month of use. Which of the following represents the relationship between the battery's capacity, C, in milliampere-hours, and the number of months, m, that the phone has been in use?

A) $C = 0.02m + 2675$

B) $C = 0.98m + 2675$

C) $C = 2675(0.02)^m$

D) $C = 2675(0.98)^m$

29.

$$S(t) = 564(1.03)^t$$

A local school board created the function above to model the number of students, $S(t)$, in the high school t years from now. According to the model, by what percent is the number of students expected to increase each year?

A) 1.03%

B) 3%

C) 5.64%

D) 56.4%

30.

x	10	15	20	25
$f(x)$	100.0	90.0	81.0	72.9

The table above shows values of x and their corresponding values of $f(x)$. Which of the following types of functions best models the relationship between x and $f(x)$?

A) Increasing exponential

B) Decreasing exponential

C) Increasing linear

D) Decreasing linear

31.

A sleep doctor determined that for each year of life, the amount of sleep required by the average person per day decreased by 1%. If a newborn requires 13 hours of sleep per day, which function models the amount of sleep, S, in hours, the average person requires at x years of age.

A) $S = 13(0.01)^x$

B) $S = 13(0.1)^x$

C) $S = 13(0.99)^x$

D) $S = 13(1.01)^x$

32.

What is the y–intercept of the graph of $y = -\left(\frac{1}{2}\right)^x + 2$, in the xy-plane?

A) $(0, 0)$

B) $(0, 1)$

C) $(0, 2)$

D) $(0, 3)$

33.

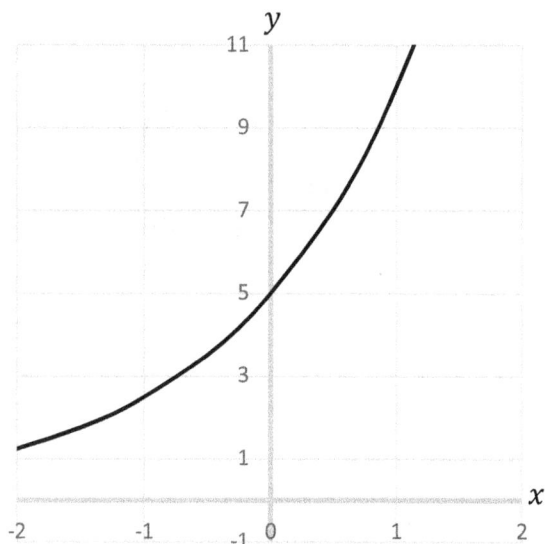

Which of the following could be the equation of the graph above?

A) $y = 2(3)^x$

B) $y = 3(2)^x$

C) $y = 4(3)^x$

D) $y = 5(2)^x$

34.

The expression $(\sqrt[3]{2})^{12}(\sqrt{4})^3$ can be rewritten as 2^n, where n is a constant. What is the value of n?

35.

If $\sqrt[3]{x^2 y^3} = y$, then what is the value of x?

A) 0

B) 1

C) 2

D) 3

36.

A wrestler wants to put on weight for an upcoming match. He currently weighs 155 pounds and wants to increase his weight by 6% in the next 7 days. Which equation represents this situation, in which w is the wrestler's weight, in pounds, and t is the number of days since he started gaining weight?

A) $w = 7(155)^{0.06t}$

B) $w = 155(1.6)^{7t}$

C) $w = 155(1.06)^{7t}$

D) $w - 155(1.06)^{\frac{t}{7}}$

37.

$$A(t) = 1000(1.03)^t$$

The function shown models the amount of money in a bank account after t years. Which of the following is the best interpretation of the number 1.03 in this context?

A) The amount of money initially deposited into the bank account.

B) The amount of time it will take the bank account to reach $1000.

C) The amount of money in the bank account will increase by a factor of 1.03 each year.

D) The amount of money in the bank account will decrease by a factor of 1.03 each year.

38.

Riley purchased a car that had a value of $8000 at the time of purchase. Each year, the car is estimated to lose 15% of its value compared to the previous year. The estimated value of the car after 5 years is given by the equation $y = 8000b$, where y is the value of the car after 5 years and b is a constant. What is the value of b, rounded to the nearest hundredth?

39.

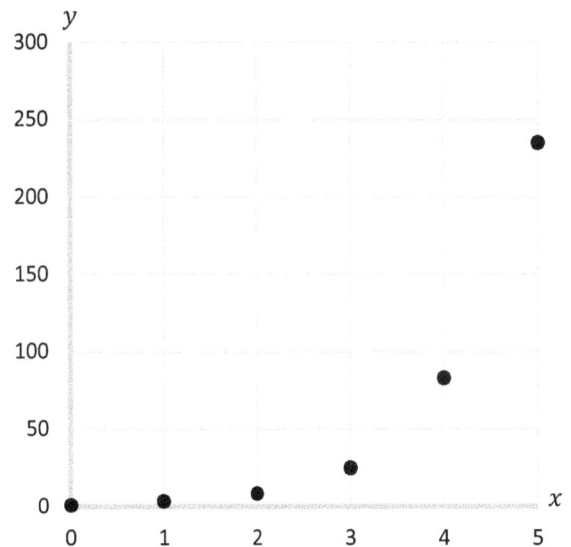

Which of the following exponential equations best models the data in the scatterplot above?

A) $y = -3^x$

B) $y = -2^x$

C) $y = 2^x$

D) $y = 3^x$

40.

The half-life of a substance, or the amount of time it takes for half of the substance to remain, is 80 years. Which of the following equations best models the amount remaining, y, of the substance, in grams, x years after there are 60 grams of the substance?

A) $y = 60(0.5)^{80x}$

B) $y = 60(0.5)^{\frac{x}{80}}$

C) $y = 80(0.5)^{60x}$

D) $y = 80(0.5)^{\frac{x}{60}}$

41.

$$\sqrt[3]{x} = y^4$$
$$x^a = y^8$$

In the system of equations above, a is a constant. If the system has an infinite number of solutions, what is the value of a?

A) $\dfrac{2}{3}$

B) $\dfrac{3}{4}$

C) $\dfrac{4}{3}$

D) $\dfrac{3}{2}$

42.

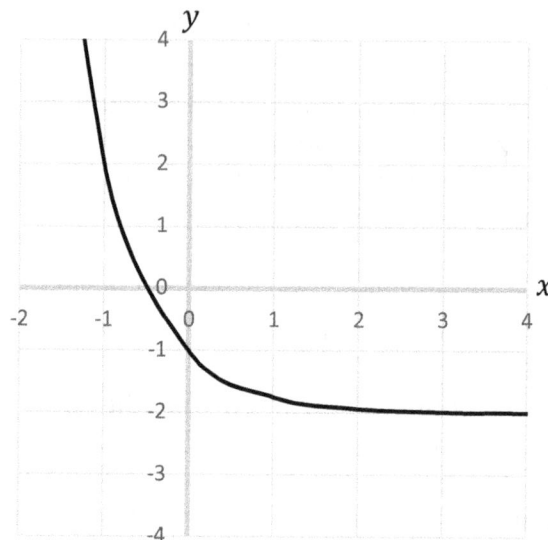

Which of the following is an equation of the graph above, in the xy-plane?

A) $y = 4^x - 2$

B) $y = 2^x - 2$

C) $y = (\frac{1}{2})^x - 2$

D) $y = (\frac{1}{4})^x - 2$

43.

$$3^{\frac{4}{a}}\left(\sqrt[a]{x^2}\right) = 9x$$

In the equation above, a is a constant. If $x > 0$, what is the value of a?

A) 1

B) 2

C) 3

D) 4

44.

A scientist prepares a petri dish with bacteria that doubles every 8 hours. If the number of bacterial cells after t hours can be modeled by the function $B(t) = 10(2)^{\frac{t}{8}}$, which of the following gives the number of bacterial cells after 2 days?

A) $B(t) = 10(2)^{\frac{1}{6}}$

B) $B(t) = 10(2)^2$

C) $B(t) = 10(2)^6$

D) $B(t) = 10(2)^{48}$

45.

$$B(t) = 15(0.5)^{\frac{t}{5}}$$

Half-life is the amount of time it takes the original quantity of a substance to decrease by half. The equation above models the half-life of bismuth-210, where $B(t)$ is the amount of bismuth remaining after t days. Which of the following is the best interpretation of the number 5 in the exponent $\frac{t}{5}$ in this context?

A) The amount of bismuth remaining after t days.

B) The amount of bismuth that has decreased after t days.

C) The number of days it takes for the bismuth to decrease by half.

D) The number of times per day that the bismuth decreases by half.

46.

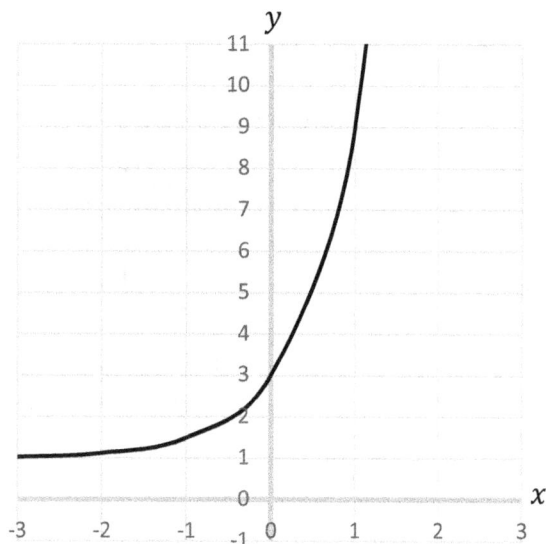

Which of the following could be the equation of the graph above?

A) $y = 2^x + 2$

B) $y = 3(2)^x$

C) $y = 4(2)^x - 1$

D) $y = 2(4)^x + 1$

47.

$$W(t) = 15(1.34)^t$$

The function above gives the estimated weight of a mole, $W(t)$, in pounds, based on its age, t, in years. Which of the following is the best interpretation of the number 1.34 in this context?

A) For each additional year of life, the mole gains an estimated 1.34 pounds.

B) For each additional 1.34 years of life, the mole gains an estimated one pound.

C) For each additional pound of weight, the estimated age of the mole increases by 34%.

D) For each additional year of life, the estimated weight of the mole increases by 34%.

48.

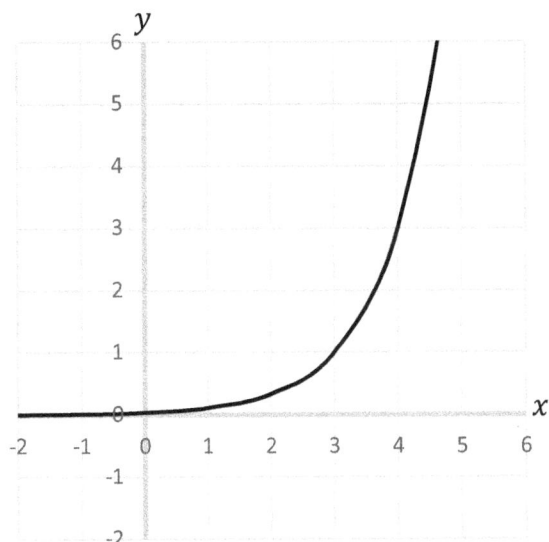

The graph above in the xy-plane is defined by $f(x) = 3^{x-h}$, in which h is a constant. What is the value of h?

A) -3

B) -2

C) 2

D) 3

49.

A stream was found to be polluted by a local factory. The amount of a certain contaminant in the stream is reduced by half every day. If the original mass, in milligrams, of the contaminant in the stream is A_0, which of the following equations gives the amount of the contaminant, C, in milligrams, in the stream in w weeks?

A) $C = A_0\left(\frac{1}{7}\right)^{\frac{w}{2}}$

B) $C = A_0\left(\frac{1}{7}\right)^{2w}$

C) $C = A_0\left(\frac{1}{2}\right)^{\frac{w}{7}}$

D) $C = A_0\left(\frac{1}{2}\right)^{7w}$

50.

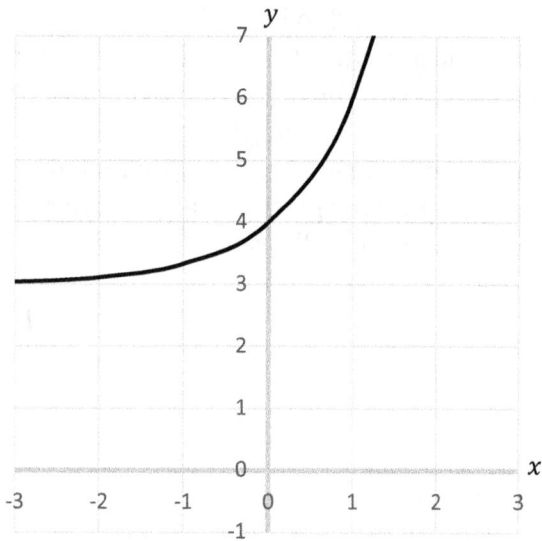

The equation of the graph above is
$y = 3^x + k$, where k is a constant. What is the value of k?

A) 1

B) 2

C) 3

D) 4

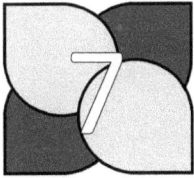

Geometry

REFERENCE

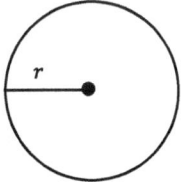

$$A = \pi r^2$$

$$C = 2\pi r$$

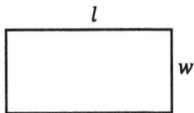

$$A = lw$$

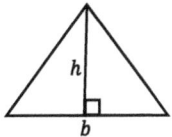

$$A = \frac{1}{2}bh$$

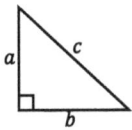

$$a^2 + b^2 = c^2$$

Special Right Triangles

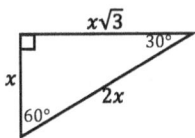

3D Volumes

Rectangular Prism: $V = lwh$

Cylinder: $V = \pi r^2 h$

Sphere: $V = \frac{4}{3}\pi r^3$

Cone: $V = \frac{1}{3}\pi r^2 h$

Pyramid: $V = \frac{1}{3}lwh$

The number of degrees of arc in a circle is 360.

The number of radians of arc in a circle is 2π.

The sum of the measures in degrees of the angles of a triangle is 180.

1.

In right triangle ABC, $\angle B$ is a right angle. If $\angle A = 25°$, what is the measure of angle C, in degrees?

A) 25

B) 35

C) 65

D) 155

2.

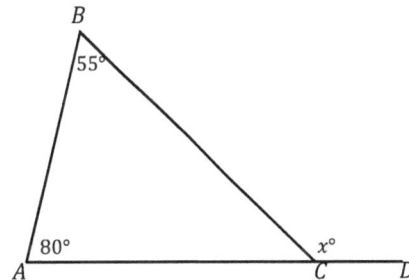

In the figure above, points A, C, and D lie on the same line. What is the value of x?

A) 45

B) 125

C) 135

D) 145

3.

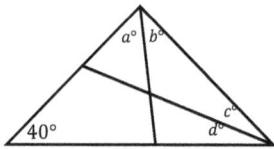

In the triangle above, what is the value of $a + b + c + d$?

A) 100

B) 120

C) 140

D) 160

4.

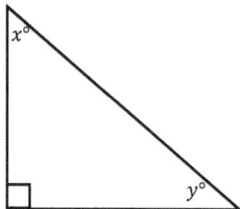

In the right triangle above, if $\tan x = \frac{4}{3}$, what is $\cos y$?

5.

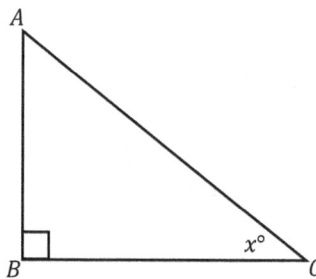

Note: Figure not drawn to scale

In the right triangle ABC above, $\overline{AC} = 16$ and $\overline{AB} = 8\sqrt{3}$. What is the value of x?

6.

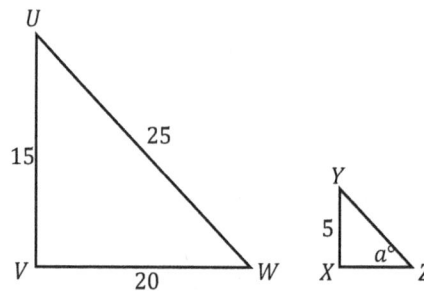

Note: Figure not drawn to scale

Triangles UVW and XYZ, shown above, are similar. If the measure of $\angle Z$ is $a°$, what is the measure of $\angle W$, in terms of a?

A) a

B) $2a$

C) $3a$

D) $4a$

7.

In the figure above, $\overline{AB} = 10$, $\overline{ED} = 12$, and $\overline{BD} = 8$. What is the perimeter of parallelogram $ACDE$, rounded to the nearest tenth?

8.

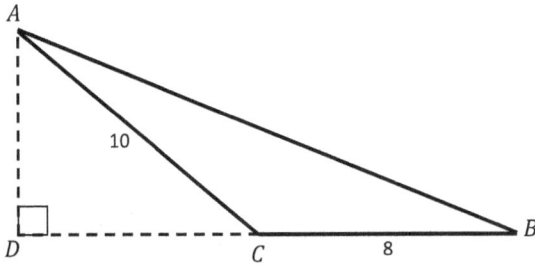

In the figure above the length of $DC = CB = 8$, and B, C, and D lie on the same line. What is the area of triangle ACB?

A) 24

B) 30

C) 40

D) 48

9.

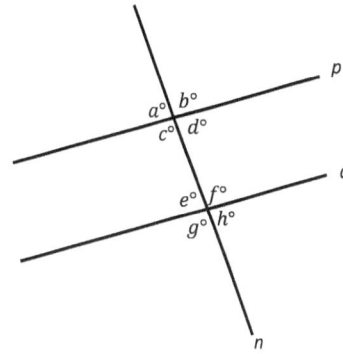

In the figure above, line p is parallel to line q. Which of the following is NOT true?

A) $a = d$

B) $b = g$

C) $b + h = 180$

D) $a + e = 180$

10.

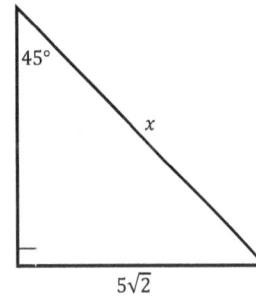

The hypotenuse of the right triangle above is x. What is the value of x?

11.

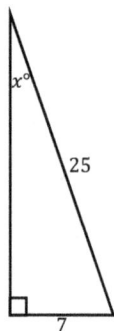

In the right triangle shown above, what is the value of tan x ?

A) $\frac{7}{25}$

B) $\frac{7}{24}$

C) $\frac{24}{25}$

D) $\frac{24}{7}$

12.

A right circular cylinder has a height of 4 and a radius of the base of r. If the volume of the cylinder is 36π, what is the value of r?

A) 3

B) 6

C) 9

D) 12

13.

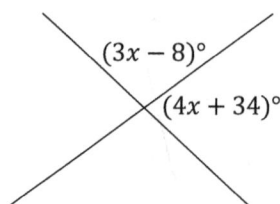

Note: Figure not drawn to scale

Two lines intersect as shown. What is the value of x?

A) 20

B) 22

C) 24

D) 26

14.

In right triangle ABC, angle B is the right angle. If $\tan A = \frac{3}{4}$, what is the value of $\sin C$?

A) $\frac{3}{5}$

B) $\frac{3}{4}$

C) $\frac{4}{5}$

D) $\frac{4}{3}$

15.

Triangle ABC is similar to triangle DEF, in which $\angle A$ corresponds to $\angle D$ and $\angle B$ corresponds to $\angle E$. If $\angle A = 22°$ and $\angle B = 79°$, what is the measure of $\angle F$?

16.

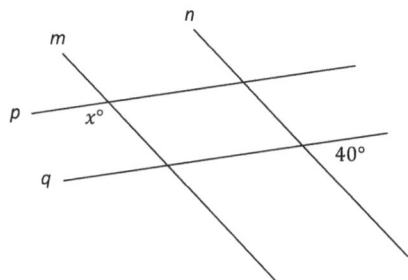

In the figure above, line m is parallel to line n and line p is parallel to line q. What is the value of x?

A) 100

B) 120

C) 140

D) 160

17.

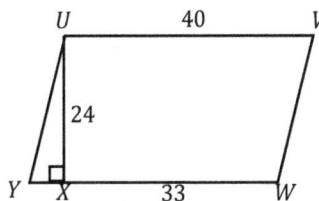

In the figure above, $UVWY$ is a parallelogram. If $\overline{UV} = 40$, $\overline{XW} = 33$, and $\overline{UX} = 24$, what is the perimeter of parallelogram $UVWY$?

A) 116

B) 123

C) 128

D) 130

18.

The height of a cone is 3 times the length of the radius of its base. Which of the following represents the cone's volume, V, in terms of its height, h?
(The volume of a cone is $\frac{1}{3}\pi r^2 h$)

A) $V = \frac{1}{27}\pi h^3$

B) $V = \frac{1}{9}\pi h^3$

C) $V = \pi h^3$

D) $V = 3\pi h^3$

19.

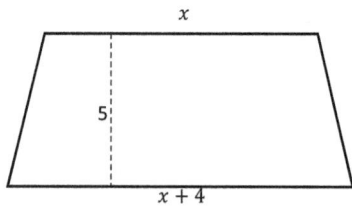

A trapezoid above has bases of x inches and $x + 4$ inches and a height of 5 inches. If the trapezoid has an area of 60 square inches, what is the length of the longer of the two bases?

A) 10

B) 12

C) 14

D) 16

20.

The dimensions of a rectangular box are 3 centimeters by 4 centimeters by 2 centimeters. What is the surface area, in square centimeters, of the box?

A) 24

B) 26

C) 48

D) 52

21.

A circle is inscribed in a square with side length of 6. If the area of the circle can be expressed a $n\pi$, what is the value of n?

A) 3

B) 6

C) 9

D) 12

22.

In the right triangle XYZ, the length of side $\overline{XY}$ is 8, the measure of $\angle X$ is 60°, and $\angle Y$ is the right angle. What is the length of side $\overline{YZ}$?

A) 4

B) $4\sqrt{3}$

C) $8\sqrt{3}$

D) 16

23.

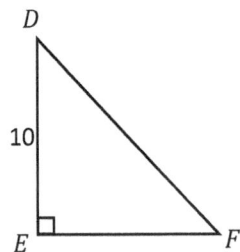

Which of the following additional pieces of information would be sufficient to determine the area of triangle DEF?

    I. The length of $\overline{EF}$
    II. The length of $\overline{DF}$
    III. The measure of $\angle EDF$

A) I only

B) Either I or II

C) III only

D) Either I, II, or III

24.

$$(x - 3)^2 + (y + 2)^2 = 49$$

The graph of the equation above is a circle in the xy-plane. What is the radius of the circle?

25.

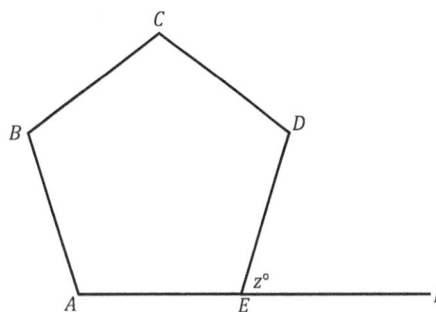

In the figure above, side AE of regular pentagon $ABCDE$ is extended to point F. What is the value of z?

A) 60

B) 72

C) 80

D) 82

26.

A small cubic box has a volume of 6 cubic feet. A larger rectangular box has dimensions of 2 yards by 3 yards by 4 yards. What is the maximum number of small boxes that can fit into the large box? (1 yard = 3 feet)

A) 4

B) 12

C) 48

D) 108

27.

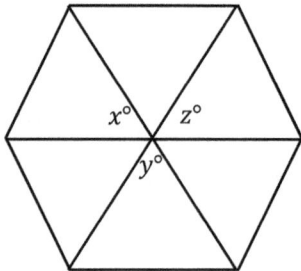

In the regular hexagon above, the lines bisect each interior angle of the hexagon. What is the value $x + y + z$?

A) 60

B) 120

C) 145

D) 180

28.

In triangle PQR, the measure of angle Q is $90°$. If $\tan P = \frac{12}{5}$, what is the length of side $\overline{PR}$?

A) 4

B) 5

C) 12

D) 13

29.

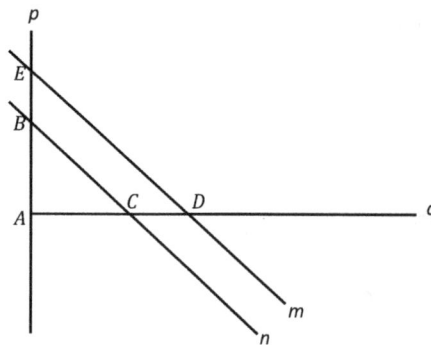

In the figure above, line p is perpendicular to line q, and line m is parallel to line n. If $\overline{AD} = 6$, $\overline{AB} = 4$, and $\angle ABC = 45°$, what is the area of triangle AED?

A) 16

B) 17

C) 18

D) 19

30.

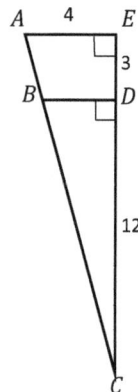

In the figure above, $\overline{AE} = 4, \overline{ED} = 3$, and $\overline{DC} = 12$. What is the length of $\overline{BD}$?

31.

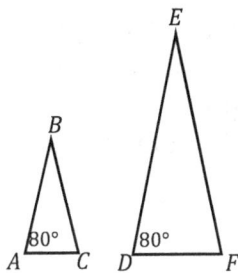

Triangles ABC and DEF shown above each have an angle of 80°. Which additional piece of information is sufficient to determine whether triangle ABC is similar to triangle DEF?

A) The measures of angles B and C

B) The length of line segments BC and EF

C) The measures of angles C and E

D) The length of line segments AC and DE

32.

The area of a square rug is 144 square feet. Each side of the rug has a length of $x - 3$ feet. Which of the following equations could be used to find the value of x?

A) $x^2 = 135$

B) $x^2 = 153$

C) $x^2 - 6x = 135$

D) $x^2 - 6x = 153$

33.

Equilateral triangle ABC is similar to triangle DEF. If $\frac{AB}{DE} = 3$ and the area of triangle DEF is $9\sqrt{3}$, what is the area of triangle ABC?

A) $3\sqrt{3}$

B) $27\sqrt{3}$

C) $54\sqrt{3}$

D) $81\sqrt{3}$

34.

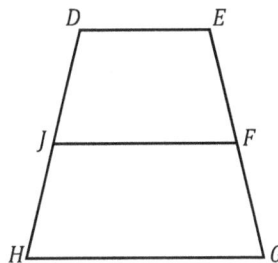

In the figure above, $\overline{DJ} = \overline{JH}, \overline{EF} = \overline{FG}$, and $\overline{DE}, \overline{JF}$, and $\overline{HG}$ are parallel. If $\overline{DE} = 11$ and $\overline{HG} = 18$, what is the length of $\overline{JF}$, to the nearest tenth?

A) 14.0

B) 14.3

C) 14.5

D) 15.2

35.

$$(x - 2)^2 + (y + 5)^2 - 7 = 42$$

The graph of the equation above is a circle in the xy-plane. What is the diameter of the circle?

36.

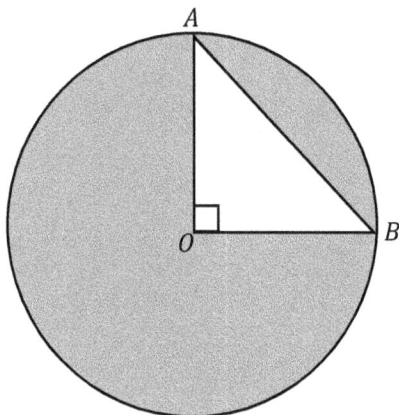

In the figure above $\overline{OA}$ and $\overline{OB}$ are radii of circle O. If the area of ΔAOB is 32, what is the area of the shaded region?

A) $16\pi - 32$

B) $32\pi - 32$

C) $64\pi - 32$

D) $128\pi - 32$

37.

The ratio of the volume of a larger cube to the volume of a smaller cube is 64 to 1. What is the ratio of the length of a side of the larger cube to the length of a side of the smaller cube?

A) 4 to 1

B) 16 to 1

C) 32 to 1

D) 64 to 1

38.

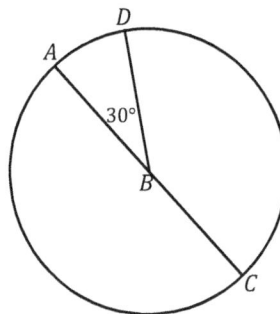

Point B is the center of the circle above and $\overline{AC}$ is a diameter of the circle. If $\overline{AC} = 12$, what is the length of arc $\overset{\frown}{DBC}$?

A) 5π

B) 10π

C) 12π

D) 15π

39.

The diameter of the base of a right circular cylinder is half the height of the cylinder. Which of the following expressions gives the volume of the cylinder in terms of its height, h?

(Volume of a cylinder is $\pi r^2 h$)

A) $\dfrac{\pi h^3}{16}$

B) $\dfrac{\pi h^3}{4}$

C) $4\pi h^3$

D) $16\pi h^3$

40.

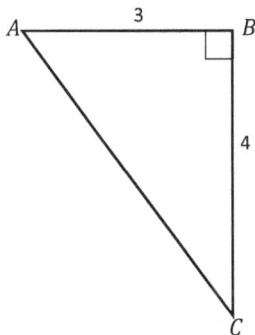

In the right triangle above, the hypotenuse can be represented by the expression $\dfrac{x}{\cos A}$. What is the value of x?

41.

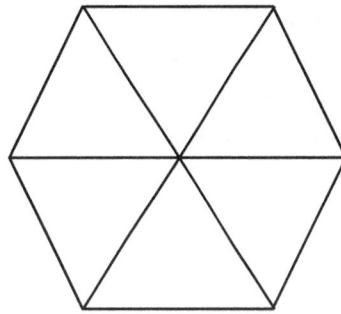

A regular hexagon can be divided into six equilateral triangles, as shown above. If the area of one of the triangles is $4\sqrt{3}$, what is the perimeter of the hexagon?

42.

$$x^2 + y^2 - 6x - 2y + 5 = 2$$

In the xy-plane, the graph of the equation above is a circle with center (a, b). What is the value of a?

A) -3

B) -1

C) 1

D) 3

43.

Sphere *A* has a radius 4 times as large as the radius of sphere *B*. Which of the following correctly expresses the ratio of the surface area of sphere *A* to the surface area of sphere *B*? (The surface area of a sphere with radius *r* is $4\pi r^2$)

A) 4 to 1

B) 16 to 1

C) 32 to 1

D) 64 to 1

44.

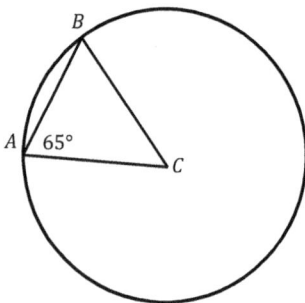

Both $\overline{AC}$ and $\overline{BC}$ are radii of the circle with center *C* above. What fraction of the circumference of the circle is arc $\overparen{AB}$?

45.

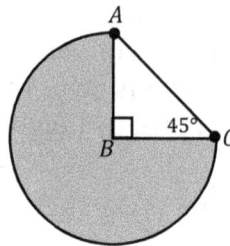

Line segments *AB* and *BC* in right triangle *ABC* are also radii of the circle with center *B*. If $\overline{AC} = 6\sqrt{2}$, what is the area of the shaded region?

A) 9π

B) 12π

C) 27π

D) 36π

46.

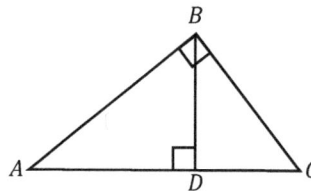

In the figure above, $\overline{AD} = 4$ and $\overline{BD} = 3$. What is the length of segment $\overline{DC}$?

A) $\frac{7}{4}$

B) 2

C) $\frac{9}{4}$

D) $\frac{5}{2}$

47.

$$x^2 + 12x + y^2 - 4y = -24$$

The graph in the xy-plane of the equation above is a circle with a radius of a. What is the value of a?

48.

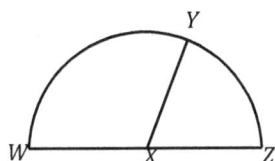

The line segments XY, XW, and XZ are each a radius of the semicircle shown above. If the area of the semicircle is 18π and $\angle WXY = 130°$, what is the length of arc $\widehat{YZ}$?

A) $\frac{5}{6}\pi$

B) $\frac{5}{3}\pi$

C) $\frac{5}{2}\pi$

D) 5π

49.

$$2x^2 + 20x + 2y^2 + 8y - 14 = 0$$

The graph in the xy-plane of the equation above is a circle. What are the coordinates of the center of the circle?

A) $(-5, -2)$

B) $(5, 2)$

C) $(-10, -4)$

D) $(10, 4)$

50.

A circle in the xy-plane has a center at $(2, 3)$ and the point $(6, 0)$ lies on the circle. If the point $(1, y)$ is also on the circle and $y > 0$, what is the value of y, rounded to the nearest tenth?

A) 7.5

B) 7.7

C) 7.9

D) 8.1

Statistics

1.

The list of numbers below represents the number of goals scored by a high school soccer team in its last 8 games:

$$5, 3, 4, 7, 6, 6, 8, 2$$

What is the median number of goals scored for these 8 games?

A) 5

B) 5.5

C) 6

D) 6.5

2.

Cost of 1GB Mobile Data

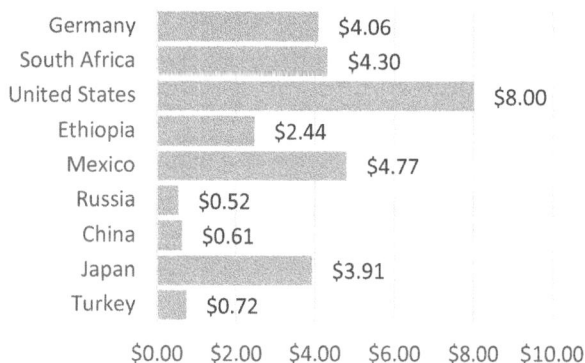

Country	Cost
Germany	$4.06
South Africa	$4.30
United States	$8.00
Ethiopia	$2.44
Mexico	$4.77
Russia	$0.52
China	$0.61
Japan	$3.91
Turkey	$0.72

$0.00 $2.00 $4.00 $6.00 $8.00 $10.00

The graph above shows the cost of 1GB of mobile data for nine countries worldwide in 2020. What was the cost, in dollars, of the country that had the median cost for 1GB of mobile data?

3.

A supermarket manager analyzed the shopping times of customers at his supermarket. He estimated that a customer's mean shopping time was 34 minutes with a margin of error of 4 minutes. Which of the following is the most accurate interpretation of the results?

A) Most customers have a shopping time of at least 34 minutes.

B) Most customers have a shopping time between 30 and 38 minutes.

C) All customers have a shopping time of between 30 and 38 minutes.

D) Customers at the supermarket have a mean shopping time between 30 and 38 minutes.

4.

$$14, 16, 4, 32, 24, 8, 42$$

What is the mean of the data set above?

A) 18

B) 20

C) 22

D) 24

5.

# of guests	5 or fewer	Between 5 and 10	10 or more
# of respondents	405	244	321

A researcher asked a random sample of 970 adult homeowners how many guests they expect to have at their next holiday gathering. The results of the survey are in the table above. If the researcher chooses one of the respondents at random, what is the probability, to the nearest hundredth, that the respondent expects to have at least 10 guests at their next holiday gathering?

A) 0.25

B) 0.33

C) 0.49

D) 0.79

6.

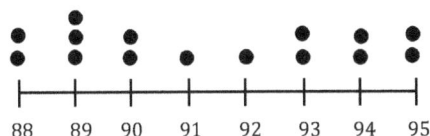

The dot plot above shows the scores of 15 different students on a science test. What is the median score for these 15 students?

A) 90

B) 91

C) 92

D) 93

7.

Two hundred Bloomfield residents will be selected for a survey about how to spend school district funds. Which of the following methods of choosing residents will provide a random sample of residents of Bloomfield?

A) Select 200 residents from shoppers at the local supermarket.

B) Select 200 residents who volunteer to take part in the survey.

C) Select 200 residents with children in the school district.

D) Select 200 residents randomly from a list of all residents of Bloomfield.

8.

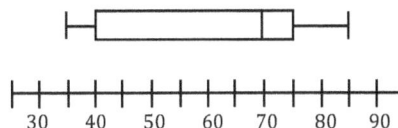

The number of customers at a coffee shop for each day in the month of March in 2019 is summarized in the box plot above. Which of the following is the closest to the median number of daily customers at the coffee shop in March 2019?

A) 35

B) 40

C) 70

D) 75

9.

Score range	Number of students
50 to 59	45
60 to 69	145
70 to 79	223
80 to 89	534
90 to 100	127

The scores on a final exam for 1,074 students at a large university are summarized in the table above. What score range contains the median score for this final exam?

A) 60 to 69

B) 70 to 79

C) 80 to 89

D) 90 to 100

10.

Set A: 2, 8, 8, 8, 9

Set A is shown above. Which of the following statements is true about set A?

A) The mean of set A is equal to the median of set A.

B) The median of set A is equal to the range of set A.

C) The mean of set A is equal to the range of set A.

D) The mean of set A is greater than the median of set A.

11.

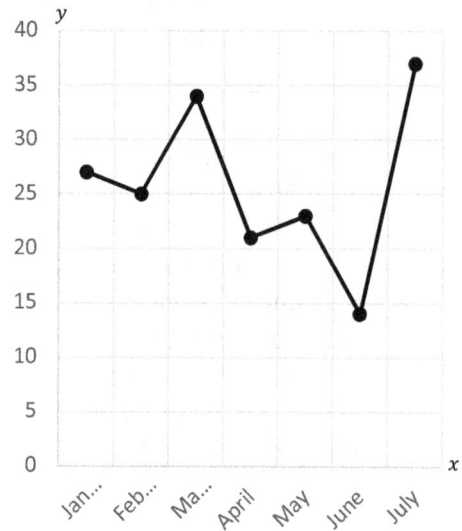

The graph above shows the number of microwaves sold at a store for each of the first 7 months of 2019. What was the median number of microwaves sold for those 7 months?

A) 21

B) 23

C) 25

D) 27

12.

Number	Frequency
1	12
2	11
3	6
4	17
5	3
6	2

The table above shows how often 6 different values appear in a data set of 61 numbers. What is the median value of the data set?

A) 2

B) 3

C) 4

D) 5

13.

A single digit positive integer is chosen at random. If the number is even, what is the probability that the number is also a multiple of 3?

A) $\frac{1}{10}$

B) $\frac{1}{5}$

C) $\frac{1}{4}$

D) $\frac{1}{3}$

14.

What is the probability that a number from 1 to 30, inclusive, is a multiple of 4?

A) $\frac{1}{5}$

B) $\frac{7}{30}$

C) $\frac{4}{15}$

D) $\frac{3}{10}$

15.

A teacher asked all 31 students in her class how many people live in their house. The results are shown in the table below.

# of People in Household	Frequency
2	1
3	8
4	11
5	4
6	5
7 or more	2

If a student is chosen at random, what is the probability that the student lives in a house with 5 or more people?

A) $\frac{7}{31}$

B) $\frac{7}{24}$

C) $\frac{11}{31}$

D) $\frac{11}{20}$

16.

A school administrator wants to understand the popularity of a new student dress code proposal. Which of the following survey designs is most likely to provide the most accurate results?

A) Surveying 500 randomly selected students nationwide.

B) Surveying 200 students in the school who volunteered to participate in the survey.

C) Surveying 200 randomly selected students in the school from a list of spring sports participants.

D) Surveying 100 randomly selected students from a list of all students in the school.

17.

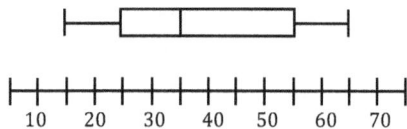

If R is the range of the data shown in the box and whisker plot and M is the median of the data shown in the box and whisker plot, what is the value of $R - M$?

A) 15

B) 20

C) 25

D) 30

18.

Frank has 5 gold coins. With a recent increase in the price of an ounce of gold, each coin's value has increased by $15. Which of the following is NOT true?

A) The new mean value of the five coins has increased by $15.

B) The standard deviation of the value of the five coins is the same as the previous standard deviation.

C) The range of values of the five coins is the same as the previous range of values of the coins.

D) The median value of the five coins is the same as the previous median value of the coins.

19.

2012	2013	2014	2015	2016	2017	2018
32.1	23.4	33.5	34.7	29.4	31.2	38.8

The number of attendees, in thousands, that visited a state fair each year from 2012 to 2018 are shown in the table above. If A is the average number of attendees, in thousands, that visited the state fair during those years and M is the median number of attendees, in thousands that visited the state fair during those years, what is the value of $M - A$, rounded to the nearest tenth?

20.

The table below shows the number of three different types of fish caught in April at two lakes: Spring Lake and Foster Lake.

	Sturgeon	Trout	Sunfish	**Total**
Spring	34	67	22	123
Foster	12	35	4	51
Total	46	102	26	174

If a fisherman caught a fish at Foster Lake in April, what is the probability that the fish he caught was a trout?

A) 0.20

B) 0.30

C) 0.34

D) 0.69

21.

Each integer from 100 to 999 is written on identical pieces of paper. One piece of paper is then chosen at random. What is the probability that the piece of paper has a number less than 400 written on it?

A) $\frac{2}{9}$

B) $\frac{1}{3}$

C) $\frac{4}{9}$

D) $\frac{2}{3}$

22.

The distribution of the results of a recent exam are below.

Score range	# of students
60-69	4
70-79	12
80-89	16
90-100	7
Total	39

Which of the following could be the median score of the 39 students who took the exam?

A) 76

B) 78

C) 82

D) 90

23.

	Black	White
Hat	4	12
Shirt	6	8

The table above shows the distribution of certain items sold at a local clothing store. If a hat is chosen at random, what is the probability it is white?

A) $\frac{12}{30}$

B) $\frac{8}{20}$

C) $\frac{12}{20}$

D) $\frac{12}{16}$

24.

Data set M

Data set N

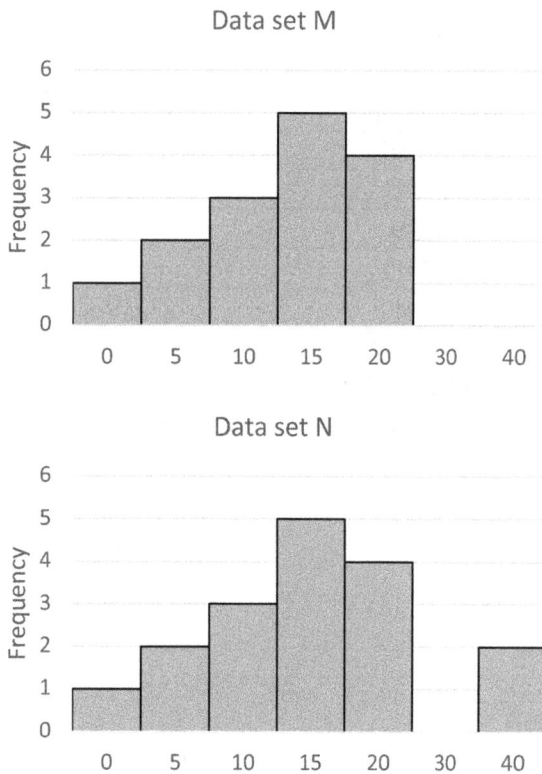

The two histograms above show the distribution of two data sets, M and N. Which of the following statements about the data sets is true?

A) The means of the data sets are the same.

B) The medians of the data sets are the same.

C) The range of the data sets is the same.

D) No comparison about the mean, median, or range can be made from the given information.

25.

Group	# of campers	Minimum age	Maximum age	Average age
A	24	6	14	9.6
B	32	7	16	8.8

At a summer camp, the campers are split up into two groups, group A and group B. If a camper is selected at random, what is the probability that the camper is from group A?

A) $\frac{3}{7}$

B) $\frac{4}{7}$

C) $\frac{3}{4}$

D) $\frac{6}{7}$

26.

$$5, 6, 11, 2, 4, 13, 8, 9$$

A data set consists of the 8 numbers shown above. A new data set is created using all 8 numbers above and an additional value, x. For which of the following values of x will the median value of the new data set remain the same?

A) 5

B) 6

C) 7

D) 8

27.

Lake	Species A	Species B	Total
Round	12	16	28
Long	3	5	8

Two invasive species of plants, species A and species B, have been spotted in two local lakes, Round Lake and Long Lake. A local crew has begun to remove these plants and record the number of plants removed from each lake. The table above shows the number of each plant that has been removed. If one removed plant is selected at random, what is the probability, rounded to the nearest tenth, that it is species A?

A) 0.1

B) 0.2

C) 0.4

D) 0.5

28.

A veterinarian weighs the 15 dogs that are in his care. He finds the mean weight of the 15 dogs is 22.4 pounds. Because of the accuracy of the scale used, there is an associated margin of error of 0.5 pounds. Which of the following is the best interpretation of the results?

A) All dogs in the veterinarian's care have a weight between 21.9 pounds and 22.9 pounds.

B) Most dogs in the veterinarian's care have a weight between 21.9 pounds and 22.9 pounds.

C) Some dogs in the veterinarian's care have a weight between 21.9 and 22.9 pounds.

D) The average weight of the dogs in the veterinarian's care is between 21.9 and 22.9 pounds.

29.

	Pine	Oak	Spruce	Total
North	122	13	15	150
South	9	76	22	107
Total	131	89	37	257

The table above shows the distribution of three different types of trees in the north and south parts of a certain town. If a tree from the north part of town is randomly selected, what is the probability that it is a spruce tree?

A) $\frac{15}{257}$

B) $\frac{37}{257}$

C) $\frac{15}{150}$

D) $\frac{37}{150}$

30.

Of 10 houses recently sold in a city, 7 sold for between $100,000 and $125,000, 2 sold for between $125,000 and $150,000, and one sold for $4,500,000. Which of the following statements about the mean and median of the sales prices of the 10 houses is true?

A) The median is greater than the mean.

B) The mean is greater than the median.

C) The mean and the median are equal.

D) There is not enough information to determine whether the median or the mean is greater.

31.

Data Set A

Data Set B

Data Set C

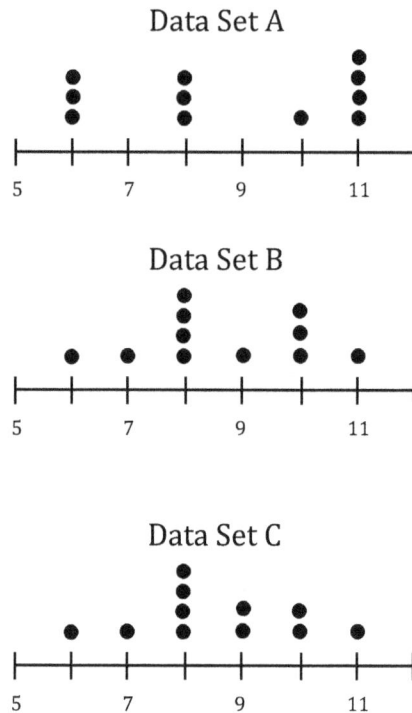

Three data sets are represented by the dot plots shown above. Which of the following statements about the data sets is true?

A) The median and the range of each data set are the same.

B) The median of each data set is the same, but the range of each data set is different.

C) The range of each data set is the same, but the median of each data set is different.

D) The range and the median of each data set are different.

32.

Goals	Frequency
2	2
3	3
4	6
5	3
6	1

An ice hockey team has played 15 games this season. The frequency table summarizes the number of goals scored in each of the 15 games. If in the 16th game, the ice hockey team scores 8 goals, how will this affect the mean and the median number of goals scored for the ice hockey team?

A) The mean and the median will both increase.

B) The mean and the median will both decrease.

C) The mean will increase, but the median will remain the same.

D) The mean will increase, but the median will decrease.

33.

Out of the 500 students in a school auditorium, 135 students are wearing red shirts, some students are wearing blue shirts, and the rest are wearing neither red shirts nor blue shirts. If the probability is $\frac{1}{20}$ that a student picked at random in the auditorium is wearing a blue shirt, what is the probability that a student is wearing neither a blue shirt nor a red shirt?

34.

Data set A

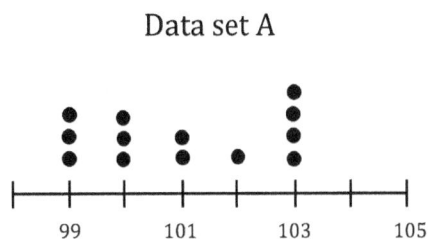

Data set A is shown in the dot plot above. Data set B is identical to data set A, except for the addition of the data point 105. Which of the following will be the same for both data sets?

    I.   median
    II. mean
    III. range

A) I only

B) I and II only

C) I and III only

D) Neither I, II, nor III

35.

Stavros has an average of 87 on his first three tests in his math class. If he wants to bring his average up to a 90 for the first four math tests, what does he need to score on the 4th math test?

A) 90

B) 93

C) 96

D) 99

36.

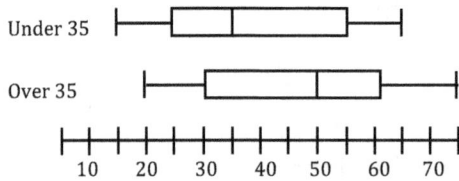

A psychologist administered a cognitive test to 100 people under 35 years of age and to 100 people over 35 years of age. The test consisted of 80 questions. The number of questions answered correctly by both groups is summarized in the box plots shown above. How much greater is the median number of questions answered correctly for the over 35 group than the median number of questions answered correctly for the under 35 group?

A) 5

B) 10

C) 15

D) 20

37.

To measure the popularity of using tax dollars to build a new park, a local mayor conducted three studies:

> I. 100 residents were selected at random from a list of all residents of the town.
> II. 200 residents were selected at random from a list of all residents of the town.
> III. 300 residents were selected at random on one afternoon during a local concert performance.

Which of the studies can be used to generalize the data to all residents of the town?

A) Study II only

B) Study III only

C) Studies I and II only

D) Studies I, II, and III

38.

$$A: \{8,8,10,12,13,14\}$$
$$B: \{8,9,10,11,12\}$$

Two sets, A and B, are shown above. If a number from set A is selected at random, what is the probability that it is also in set B?

A) $\dfrac{1}{2}$

B) $\dfrac{3}{5}$

C) $\dfrac{2}{3}$

D) $\dfrac{4}{5}$

39.

A pollster conducted two different polls to gauge the popularity of a local politician. In poll A, he found that 62% of the residents had a favorable opinion of the politician with a 4% margin of error. In poll B, he found that 68% of the residents had a favorable opinion of the politician with a 2.5% margin of error. Which of the following is the most likely reason that the margin of error is larger in the first poll?

A) Poll A was conducted earlier than poll B.

B) Poll A was conducted after poll B.

C) Poll A sampled fewer people than poll B.

D) Poll B sampled fewer people than poll A.

40.

Data set M

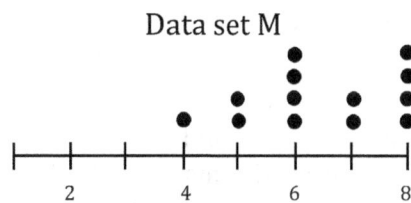

Data set N

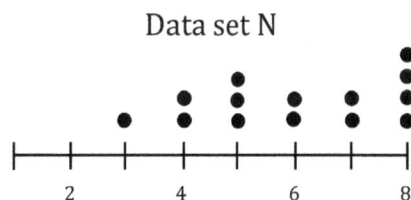

The dot plots above show two different data sets. Which of the following is true about the means of data sets M and N?

A) The mean of data set M is greater than the mean of data set N.

B) The mean of data set N is greater than the mean of data set M.

C) The mean of data set M is equal to the mean of data set N.

D) There is not enough information given to compare the means of data sets M and N.

41.

Set A: 2, 3, 4, 5, 6, 7
Set B: 5, 6, 7, 8, 9, 10, 11

Two sets of numbers are shown above. If a number is chosen at random from set B, what is the probability it is NOT also in set A?

A) $\frac{1}{3}$

B) $\frac{3}{7}$

C) $\frac{1}{2}$

D) $\frac{4}{7}$

42.

The mean height of the 12 members of a college basketball team is 81.5 inches. After one member of the team is injured, the 11 remaining members on the team have a mean height of 83 inches. How many inches tall is the injured player?

43.

Data Set A

Data Set B

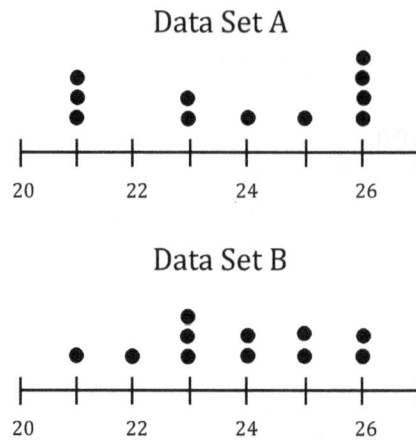

Data sets A and B are shown in the dot plots above. Which of the following is the same for both data sets?

    I.   mean
   II. median

A) I only

B) II only

C) I and II

D) Neither I nor II

44.

Set X	22	26	35	11	37	44
Set Y	2	44	166	22	254	343

Which of the following statements is true about the sets of data above?

A) The standard deviation of set X is larger than the standard deviation of set Y.

B) The standard deviation of set Y is larger than the standard deviation of set X.

C) The standard deviation of set X is equal to the standard deviation of set Y.

D) There is not enough information available to compare the standard deviations of the two data sets.

45.

For the first 9 games of the season, a high school football team averaged 24 points per game. For the first 8 games of the season, the team averaged 22 points per game. How many points were scored by the football team in the 9th game of the season?

A) 26

B) 30

C) 36

D) 40

46.

Data set P

Data set Q

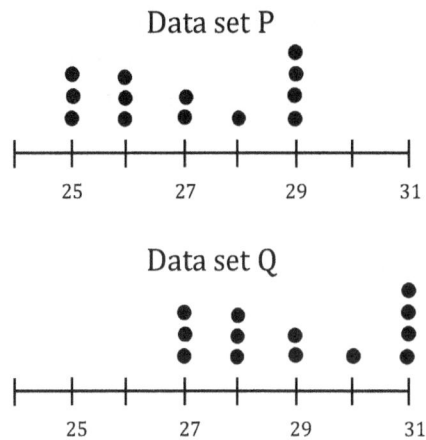

Two data sets are shown in the dot plots above. Which of the following statements is true?

A) The standard deviation of data set P is greater than the standard deviation of data set Q.

B) The standard deviation of data set Q is greater than the standard deviation of data set P.

C) The standard deviations of the data sets are the same.

D) It cannot be determined which data set has the greater standard deviation from the information given.

47.

A two-digit positive integer will be chosen at random. What is the probability that the number will have at least one 2 as a digit?

A) $\frac{9}{90}$

B) $\frac{10}{90}$

C) $\frac{18}{90}$

D) $\frac{19}{90}$

48.

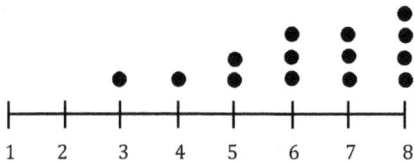

Which of the following is true about the data set represented by the dot plot above?

A) The mean of the data set is greater than the median of the data set.

B) The median of the data set is greater than the mean of the data set.

C) The mean of the data set is equal to the median of the data set.

D) There is not enough information to compare the mean and the median of the data set.

49.

Data set X

Data set Y

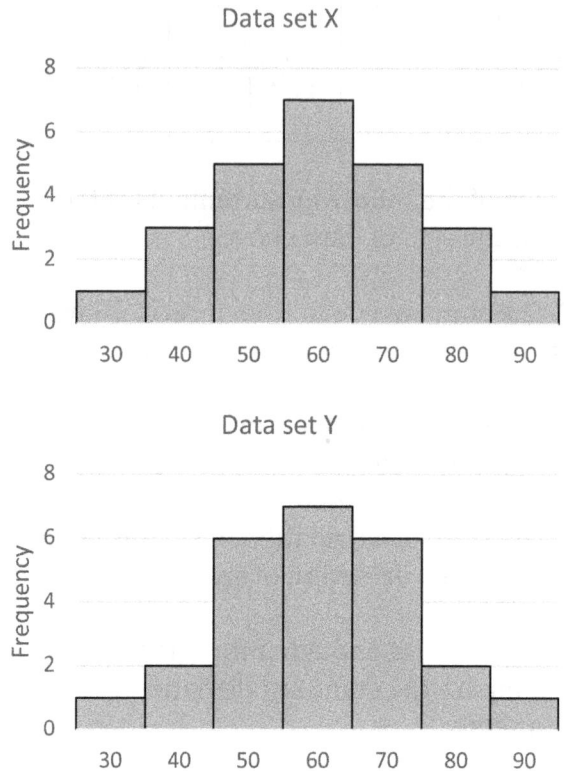

The two histograms above represent two different data sets that each have a mean of 60. Which of the following statements about the standard deviation of the data above is true?

A) The standard deviation of data set X data is greater than the standard deviation of data set Y.

B) The standard deviation of data set Y is greater than the standard deviation of data set X.

C) The standard deviation of data set X is the same as the standard deviation data set Y.

D) There is not enough information to determine whether the standard deviation of data set X is greater than the standard deviation of data set Y.

50.

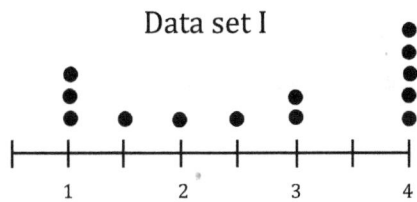

Data set I

Which of the following is true about data set I, shown in the dot plot above?

A) The mean of data set I is greater than the median of data set I.

B) The median of data set I is greater than the mean of data set I.

C) The mean of data set I is equal to the median of data set I.

D) The relationship between the mean and the median of data set I cannot be determined.

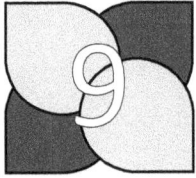

"Advanced" Math

1.

What is the sum of the complex numbers $2 - 3i^2$ and $4 + 3i^2$? (Note: $i = \sqrt{-1}$)

A) 0

B) 3

C) 6

D) 9

2.

A function is defined by the equation $f(x) = -2x^2 + 2x - 3$. What is the value of $f(-1)$?

A) −7

B) −3

C) −1

D) 1

3.

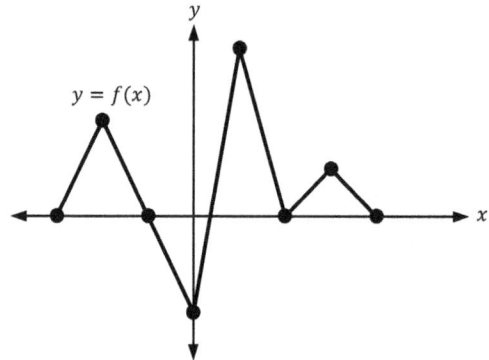

The graph of the function f is shown above in the xy-plane. For how many values of x is it true that $f(x) = 0$?

A) One

B) Two

C) Three

D) Four

4.

$$f(x) = \frac{3}{4}x + 8$$

A function f is defined by the equation above. What is the value of x when $f(x) = 20$?

A) 9

B) 12

C) 16

D) 23

5.

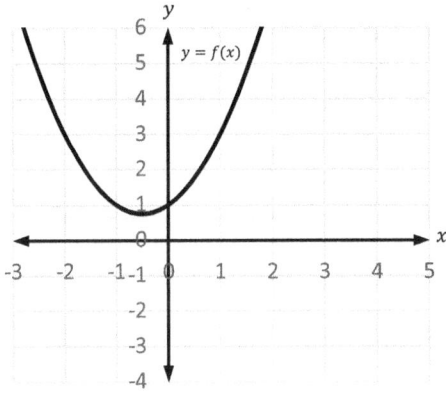

The graph of the function f is shown above in the xy-plane. If $f(-2) = f(a)$, where a is a constant, what is the value of a?

A) 0

B) 1

C) 2

D) 3

6.

$$p(x) = -x^4 - 2x^3 - 3x + 5$$

The function p is defined by the equation above. What is the value of $p(-2)$?

A) -21

B) -1

C) 11

D) 43

7.

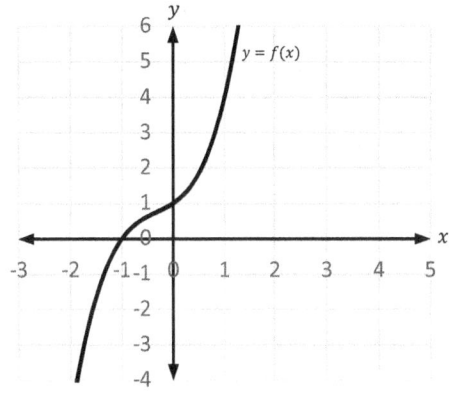

The graph of the function f is shown above in the xy-plane. What is the value of $f(1)$?

A) -1

B) 0

C) 1

D) 4

8.

What is the value of the complex number $-2i^4 + 3$? (Note: $i = \sqrt{-1}$)

A) 1

B) 2

C) 4

D) 5

9.

What is the sum of the complex numbers $2 - 3i$ and $-5 + 3i^2$? (Note: $i = \sqrt{-1}$)

A) -3

B) -9

C) $-3i$

D) $-6 - 3i$

10.

$$f(x) = (x - 3)^2 + 8$$

The function f, defined by the equation above, has a vertex at $(3, 8)$. If the function g is defined by $g(x) = f(x) - 3$, what is the y-coordinate of the vertex of the graph of $g(x)$?

11.

The graph of a function g contains the points $(1, 4)$ and $(2, 3)$. Which of the following equations CANNOT be true?

A) $f(5) = 1$

B) $f(4) = 5$

C) $f(3) = 2$

D) $f(2) = 4$

12.

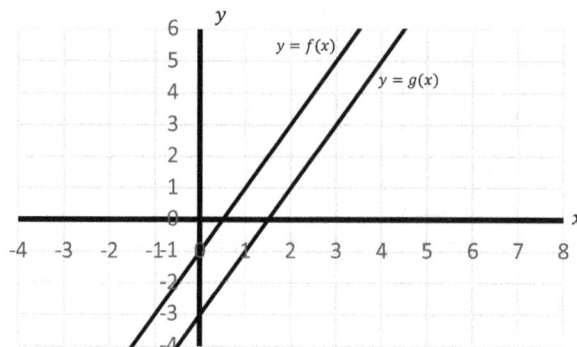

A portion of the linear functions f and g are shown above. If $g(x) = f(x + h)$, where h is a constant, what is the value of h?

A) -2

B) -1

C) 1

D) 2

13.

The measure of an angle is $\frac{5}{3}\pi$ radians. If the degree measure of the angle is d degrees, where $0 \le d < 360$, what is the value of d?

14.

$$f(x) = 2x^2 - 3$$

The function f is defined by the equation above. In the xy-plane, for how many points does $f(x) = 0$?

A) Zero

B) One

C) Two

D) Three

15.

$$f(x) = 2x - 5$$

A function f is defined by the equation above. If $f(x - 2) = 7$, what is the value of x?

A) 5

B) 6

C) 7

D) 8

16.

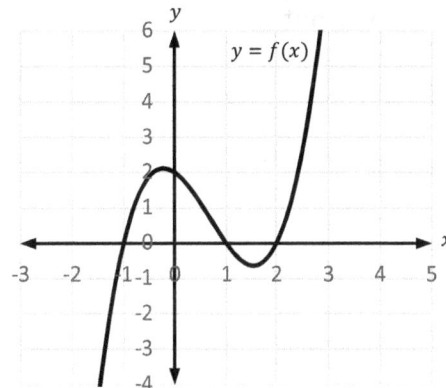

A function f is graphed above. Which of the following values of $f(x)$ has three real solutions for x?

A) -3

B) -1

C) 1

D) 3

17.

$$\frac{3 + i}{4 - 3i}$$

If the complex number above is written in the form $a + bi$, what is the value of b?

18.

If $f(x) = x^2 - 3x$, what does $f(-2x)$ equal?

A) $-4x^2 - 6x$

B) $-4x^2 + 6x$

C) $4x^2 - 6x$

D) $4x^2 + 6x$

19.

$$f(x) = (x - 2)^2 + 3$$
$$g(x) = (x + 2)^2 + 1$$

The graph of the function f is the image of the graph of the function g after which of the following translations?

A) A translation of 2 units up and 4 units to the right.

B) A translation of 2 units down and 4 units to the right.

C) A translation of 2 units up and 4 units to the left.

D) A translation of 2 units down and 4 units to the left.

20.

$$f(x) = 3x^2 - 1$$

The function f is defined above. If $f(a\sqrt{3}) = 0$, where a is a positive constant, what is the value of a?

A) $\frac{1}{9}$

B) $\frac{1}{3}$

C) 3

D) 9

21.

$$(2i - 1)(3i + 4)$$

If the complex number above is rewritten in the form $a + bi$, where a and b are constants, what is the value of a? (Note: $i = \sqrt{-1}$)

A) -10

B) -4

C) 2

D) 5

22.

The measure of an angle is 75 degrees. If the radian measure of the same angle is $r\pi$ radians, where $0 \le r \le 2$, what is the value of r?

23.

x	$f(x)$	$g(x)$
1	4	-2
2	3	-4
3	6	2
4	1	3
5	2	-6
6	-3	5

The table above shows some values for the functions f and g. According to the table, what is the value of $g(f(5))$?

A) -6

B) -4

C) -3

D) 2

24.

$$f(x) = ax^2 + 2x + c$$

In the function above, a and c are constants. If $f(2) = 6$ and $f(3) = 10$, what is the value of c?

25.

Joan is taking a vacation to a destination 450 miles from her house. The function v defined by $v(t) = 450 - 37t$ models the number of miles that Joan has left until she reaches her destination t hours after she starts driving. Which of the following is the best interpretation of $v(10) = 80$ in this context?

A) Joan has traveled 80 miles in the first 10 hours of driving.

B) After driving for 10 hours, Joan has 80 miles remaining.

C) Joan has 10 hours remaining to travel the last 80 miles.

D) After Joan has traveled for 80 miles, she has 10 hours remaining in her trip.

26.

Which of the following complex numbers is equivalent to $\frac{3}{4-i}$?

A) $\frac{4+i}{3}$

B) $\frac{4+i}{5}$

C) $\frac{12+3i}{5}$

D) $\frac{12+3i}{17}$

27.

An angle with measure d degrees has a radian measure of $\frac{4\pi}{3}$. If $0 \le d < 360$, what is the value of d?

28.

In the xy-plane, the function f is a parabola with a maximum at $(-2, 5)$. The function g can be defined by $g(x) = f(x+3) - k$, where k is a constant. If g has a graph with a maximum at $(-5, -1)$, what is the value of k?

29.

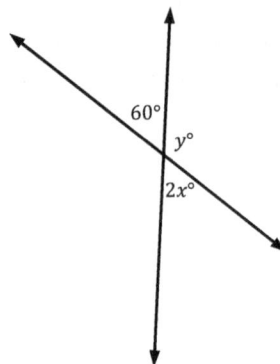

The figure above consists of two intersecting lines. What is the value of $x + y$, in radians?

A) $\frac{2}{3}\pi$

B) $\frac{5}{6}\pi$

C) π

D) $\frac{7}{6}\pi$

30.

$$f(x) = \frac{(x-2)^2 + 3}{3a}$$

In the function f defined above, a is a constant. If $f(2) = 9$, what is the value of $f(4)$?

A) $\frac{7}{9}$

B) $\frac{7}{3}$

C) 21

D) 63

31.

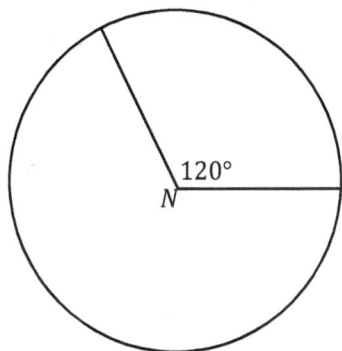

In circle N shown above, the angle with measure $120°$ has a radian measure of $x\pi$. What is the value of x?

32.

$$f(x) = ax^3$$

The function f is defined by the equation above, where a is a constant. If $f(2a^2) = f(a)$, what is the value of a?

A) $\frac{1}{16}$

B) $\frac{1}{8}$

C) $\frac{1}{4}$

D) $\frac{1}{2}$

33.

The graphs of the linear functions f and g intersect at the point $(1, 2)$. If $g(3) = -7$, what is the y-intercept of the graph of $g(x)$?

34.

$$f(x) = 2x^2 + 1$$
$$g(x) = 2 - 2f(x)$$

The functions f and g are defined above. For what value of x does $g(x) = -16$?

A) -1

B) 0

C) 1

D) 2

35.

Which of the following is equivalent to the product of the complex numbers i^3 and i^5? (Note: $i = \sqrt{-1}$)

A) $-i$

B) i

C) -1

D) 1

36.

An arc of a circle measuring 1.7 radians has an equivalent degree measure of x. To the nearest tenth of a degree, what is the value of x?

A) 97.4

B) 170.0

C) 194.8

D) 306.0

37.

$$f(x) = 2x^2 + 3$$
$$g(x) = 2x - 1$$

The functions f and g are defined by the equations above, where $x \geq 0$. If $f(g(x)) = 21$, what is the value of x?

A) 1

B) 2

C) 3

D) 4

38.

$$f(x) = 2 - x^3$$
$$g(x) = 5 - (x - 2)^3$$

The graph of the function g is the image of the graph of the function f after which of the following translations?

A) A translation of 3 units up and 2 units to the right.

B) A translation of 3 units down and 2 units to the right.

C) A translation of 3 units up and 2 units to the left.

D) A translation of 3 units down and 2 units to the left.

39.

The central angle of a circle graphed in the xy-plane has a measure of $\frac{5}{8}\pi$ radians. The sector formed by that central angle is what percent of the area of the circle? (Round your answer to the nearest percent)

40.

A function f is defined by $f(x) = |x|$ and another function g is defined by $g(x) = |x - 3| + 2$. How does the graph of the function g compare to the graph of the function f?

A) It is translated down 3 units and right 2 units.

B) It is translated up 2 units and left 3 units.

C) It is translated up 2 units and right 3 units.

D) It is translated down 3 units and left 2 units.

41.

$$f(x) = \frac{2}{3}x^2 - 3a$$

In the function above, a is a constant. If $f(3) = 0$, what is the value of $3 \cdot f(a)$?

A) -10

B) -6

C) 6

D) 10

42.

$$\frac{2i + 3}{2i - 3}$$

The complex number above can be written in the form $-\frac{5}{n} - \frac{12}{n}i$, where n is a constant. What is the value of n?

A) 4

B) 7

C) 10

D) 13

43.

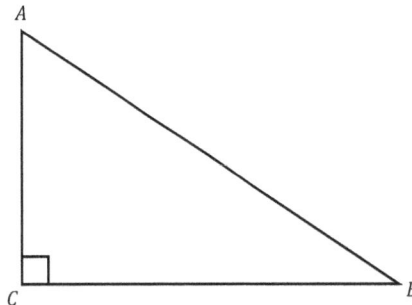

In triangle ABC above, $\angle CAB = 2 \cdot \angle ABC$. If the measure of $\angle CAB$ can be expressed as $\frac{\pi}{r}$ radians, what is the value of r?

A) 2

B) 3

C) 4

D) 6

44.

If $\sin x = \frac{\sqrt{3}}{2}$ and $\frac{\pi}{2} < x < \pi$, what is $\cos x$?

A) -2

B) $-\frac{1}{2}$

C) $\frac{1}{2}$

D) 2

45.

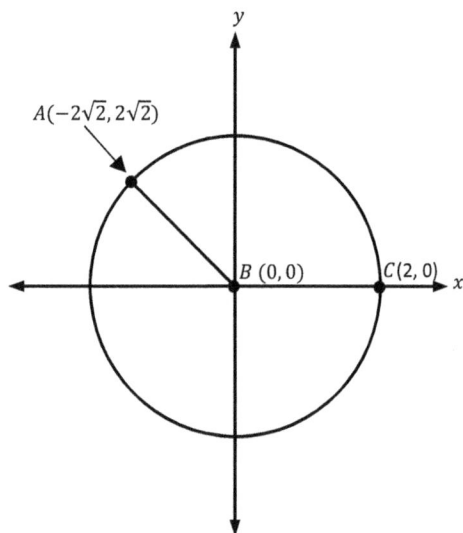

In the xy-plane above, point A with coordinates shown lies on the circle with center B. What is the measure of $\angle ABC$, in radians?

A) $\frac{2}{3}\pi$

B) $\frac{3}{4}\pi$

C) $\frac{5}{6}\pi$

D) $\frac{7}{8}\pi$

46.

$$f(x) = a^{2x}$$

In the function f above, a is a positive constant. If $f(4) = 16f(3)$, what is the value of a?

A) 2

B) 3

C) 4

D) 5

47.

Which of the following is the complex number $\frac{-2+4i}{5} + \frac{4-2i}{2+i}$ written in the form $a + bi$?

A) $\frac{4}{5} - \frac{4}{5}i$

B) $\frac{8}{5} - \frac{4}{5}i$

C) $\frac{4}{5} + \frac{4}{5}i$

D) $\frac{8}{5} + \frac{4}{5}i$

48.

$$\frac{2}{2-i} - \frac{1}{3+i}$$

The expression above can be written in the form $\frac{1+i}{a}$, where a is a constant. What is the value of a? (Note: $i = \sqrt{-1}$)

A) 1

B) 2

C) 5

D) 10

49.

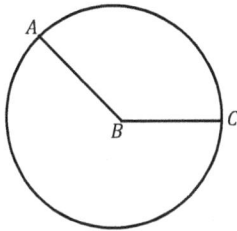

In the circle above with center B, the area of the sector formed by central angle ABC is $\frac{3}{8}$ of the area of circle B. If the radian measure of $\angle ABC$ can be written as $x\pi$, where x is a constant, what is the value of x?

50.

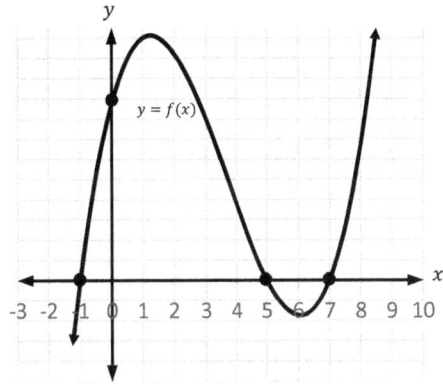

The graph of the function $f(x) = x^3 - 11x^2 + 23x + 35$ is shown above. What is the value of $f(0)$?

A) −1

B) 5

C) 9

D) 35

Final Exam

1.

$$(x - h)^2 + (y - k)^2 = r^2$$

A circle in the xy-plane is defined by the equation above, in which h, k, and r are constants. If $(2, 3)$ and $(8, 11)$ are two endpoints of a diameter of the circle, what is the value of $h + k + r$?

2.

$$2^x = 8^y$$
$$x + 3y = 12$$

If (x, y) is the solution to the system of equations above, what is the value of $x + y$?

A) 2

B) 4

C) 6

D) 8

3.

$$2(x - a)(x + b)^2 = 2x^3 + 8x^2 - 6x - 36$$

In the equation above, a and b are constants. If the equation is true for all values of x, what is the value of ab?

4.

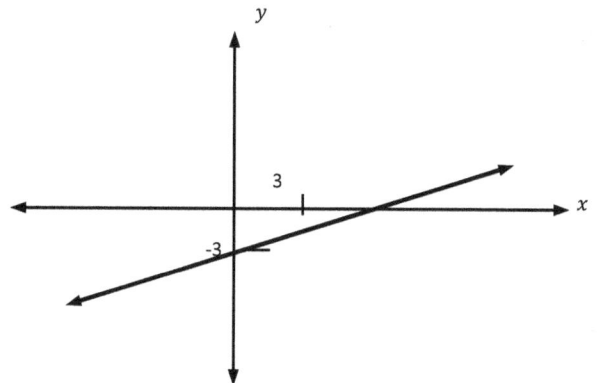

The graph above in the xy-plane has equation $y = \dfrac{a}{b}x - 3$, where a and b are negative constants. Which of the following statements about a and b is true?

A) $a > b$

B) $b > a$

C) $a = b$

D) The relationship between a and b cannot be determined from the given information.

5.

The expression $5x^2 + bx + 4$ can be rewritten as $(5x + a)(x + a)$, in which a and b are constants. What is the value of ab?

A) 12

B) 24

C) 36

D) 48

6.

$$\frac{1 + n}{2 - n} - 1$$

The expression above is equivalent to which of the following expressions?

A) $\frac{-1}{2n}$

B) $\frac{-1}{2-n}$

C) $\frac{2n-1}{2n}$

D) $\frac{2n-1}{2-n}$

7.

A number n is increased by 20%. It is then decreased by 25%. The resulting number, m, is what percent of the original number, n?

A) 90

B) 95

C) 100

D) 105

8.

The area of a square can be given by the expression $4a^2 - 16a + 16$, in which a is a constant. If the area of the square is 49, what is the value of a?

A) 5.5

B) 7.0

C) 8.5

D) 10.0

9.

$$2^{\frac{3}{t}} \cdot \sqrt[t]{8} = 4$$

In the equation above, what is the value of t?

10.

$$x^2 - 3x + 2c = 0$$

In the quadratic equation above, c is a constant. If the equation has no solutions, which of the following is a possible value of c?

A) $\frac{1}{3}$

B) $\frac{2}{3}$

C) $\frac{3}{4}$

D) $\frac{4}{3}$

11.

$$f(x) = 4(x-2)^2 + 3$$

What is the minimum value of $f(x)$ for the function f above?

A) -2

B) 2

C) 3

D) 4

12.

If the value of $f(x)$ triples whenever the value of x increases by 2, which of the following could define the function f?

A) $f(x) = 3(2)^{\frac{x}{2}}$

B) $f(x) = 2(3)^{\frac{x}{3}}$

C) $f(x) = 3(3)^{\frac{x}{2}}$

D) $f(x) = 2(3)^{x+2}$

13.

$$-\frac{3}{2}x - \frac{1}{3}y = -4$$
$$\frac{3}{4}x + by = 3$$

In the system of equations above, b is a constant. If the system of equations has no solution, what is the value of b ?

14.

$$\frac{x-2}{3} - \frac{x}{2} = \frac{x+4}{4}$$

If x is the solution to the equation above, what is the value of $|x|$?

15.

In the xy-plane, line l passes through the points $(-2, 3)$ and $(3, 4)$. Line n is perpendicular to line l and passes through the point $(5, 2)$. If an equation of line n is $y = mx + b$, what is the value of b?

16.

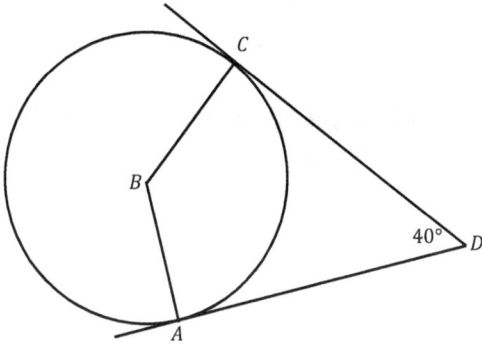

In the figure above, line segment $\overline{CD}$ is tangent to the circle with center B at point C and line segment $\overline{AD}$ is tangent to the circle at point A. If minor arc $\widehat{AC}$ has length 14π, what is the length of $\overline{AB}$?

A) 12

B) 14

C) 16

D) 18

17.

A circle in the xy-plane has a center at $(3, 7)$. If the points $(2, 4)$ and $(4, a)$ lie on the circle, what is a possible value of a?

A) 6

B) 8

C) 10

D) 12

18.

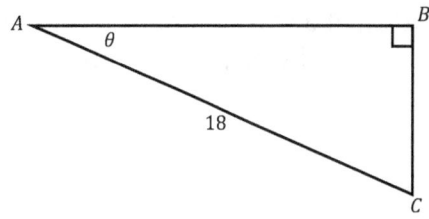

In right triangle ABC above, $\sin \theta = \frac{1}{3}$. If $\overline{AB} = a\sqrt{b}$, where a and b are integers and $a > b$, what is the value of a?

A) 2

B) 6

C) 10

D) 12

19.

Jimmy bought 5 shares of a stock. After an initial drop of 20% in the value of the stock in the first year, the stock increased by 340% in the second year. If x represents the initial price of the stock, which of the following expressions represents the price of the stock after 2 years?

A) 2.72x

B) 3.20x

C) 3.52x

D) 6.80x

20.

The height, $h(t)$, of a leaf t seconds after being blown off a tree can be modeled by the function h below:

$$h(t) = -\frac{1}{2}t^2 + 4t + 6$$

How many seconds after getting blown off the tree does the leaf reach its maximum height?

A) 4

B) 7

C) 10

D) 14

21.

$$A(t) = 2500(1.015)^{4t}$$

The equation above can be used to model the amount of money, in dollars, Gina will have t years after depositing $2500 into a bank account. If the account increases by 1.5% every m months, what is the value of m?

A) 3

B) 4

C) 15

D) 48

22.

$$7y - 2ay + b = y + 4$$

In the equation above, a and b are constants. If the equation has infinitely many solutions, what is the value of $a + b$?

23.

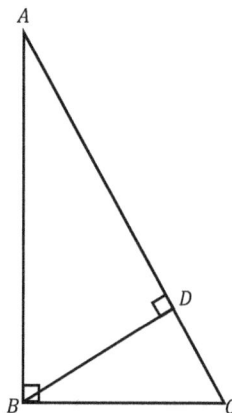

In the figure above, $\overline{BD} = 5$ and $\overline{AD} = 10$. What is the area of triangle BDC?

A) 5.00

B) 5.75

C) 6.25

D) 7.50

24.

$$\frac{(2x^{\frac{2}{3}})^3}{x^{-2}}$$

The expression above can be rewritten as $8x^b$, where b is a constant. What is the value of b?

A) 0

B) 4

C) 6

D) 8

25.

$$f(x) = (x + 2)^3(x - 1)^2(x + 3)$$

The function f is defined by the equation above. If $f(y + 3) = 0$, which of the following is a possible value of y?

A) 0

B) −1

C) −2

D) −3

26.

A three-digit integer is selected at random. What is the probability that it begins or ends in a 3?

A) $\frac{100}{900}$

B) $\frac{172}{900}$

C) $\frac{180}{900}$

D) $\frac{190}{900}$

27.

In right triangle ABC with right angle B, which of the following must be true?

A) $\sin A = \sin C$

B) $\tan A = \sin C$

C) $\cos A = \cos C$

D) $\sin A = \cos C$

28.

$$f(x) = x^2 + 3x$$

The function f is defined above. If the graph of the function contains the point $(a + 1, b + 3)$, where a and b are constants, which of the following expresses b, in terms of a?

A) $a^2 + 3a + 1$

B) $a^2 + 3a + 4$

C) $a^2 + 5a + 1$

D) $a^2 + 5a + 4$

29.

$$2x - 3y = 23$$
$$\frac{a}{4}x + 3y = 10$$

In the linear equation above, a is a constant. The graphs of the two linear equations are perpendicular lines in the xy-plane. What is the value of a?

A) 8

B) 9

C) 15

D) 18

30.

The graph of the function $f(x) = ax^3 + 2b$, where a and b are constants, contains the point $(2, 22)$. If $f(3) = 60$, what is the value of ab?

A) 2

B) 3

C) 6

D) 12

31.

The equation $3x - 12 = a(x - b)$, where a and b are constants, has no solution. Which of the following CANNOT be the value of b?

A) 3

B) 4

C) 5

D) 6

32.

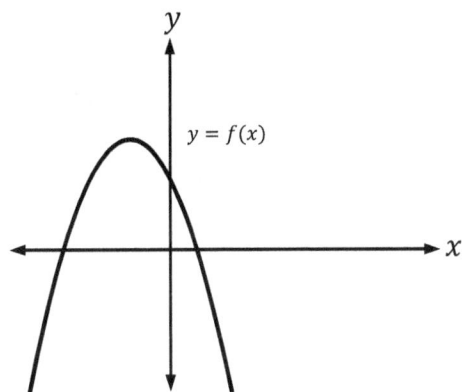

The parabola above has a vertex at $(-a, 3)$ and equation $-x^2 - bx + c$, where b and c are constants. Which of the following is a possible value of c?

A) -2

B) 2

C) 3

D) 5

33.

$$(i^3)^4$$

Which of the following is equivalent to the expression above? (Note: $i = \sqrt{-1}$)

A) 1

B) i

C) $-i$

D) i^7

34.

$$y = -ax^2 + b$$
$$y = -b$$

In the system of equations above, a and b are positive constants. How many solutions does the system of equations have?

A) Zero

B) One

C) Two

D) More than two

35.

Which of the following is equivalent to $\dfrac{1}{\dfrac{1}{2x} + \dfrac{1}{2x+1}}$?

A) $4x$

B) $4x + 1$

C) $\dfrac{4x+1}{3}$

D) $\dfrac{4x^2+2x}{4x+1}$

36.

Which of the following is the positive solution to the equation $y = (3x - 1)^2 - 6(-3x + 1)$?

A) $\frac{1}{3}$

B) $\frac{2}{3}$

C) $\frac{4}{3}$

D) $\frac{5}{3}$

37.

$$f(x) = \frac{3x + a}{2x + 4a}$$

In the function f defined above, a is a constant. If $(2, \frac{1}{2})$ is a point on the graph of f, what is the value of $f(4)$?

A) $\frac{1}{3}$

B) $\frac{2}{3}$

C) $\frac{3}{4}$

D) $\frac{7}{8}$

38.

$$(x - 2)^2 - 2(-10 - 3x) = 4x^2 - 3x + 12$$

What is the sum of the solutions to the equation above?

A) $\frac{4}{3}$

B) $\frac{5}{3}$

C) $\frac{7}{3}$

D) $\frac{9}{4}$

39.

In which of the following equations does the y-intercept of its graph in the xy-plane appear as a constant or a coefficient?

A) $y = 2x^2 - 3x - 4$

B) $y = (x - 2)^2 + 3$

C) $y = 2(3)^{x+1}$

D) $x = \frac{2}{3}y + 3$

40.

On a map, Tim measures the distance from his home to his destination to be $2\frac{3}{8}$ inches. The map says that each $\frac{1}{4}$ inch is equal to 50 miles. If Tim will travel an average of 50 miles per hour on this trip, how many minutes will it take Tim to reach his destination?

41.

$$f(x) = 2(3)^{x-4}$$

Which of the following is the x-intercept of the graph of the function f above, in the xy-plane?

A) 2

B) 3

C) 4

D) There is no x-intercept.

42.

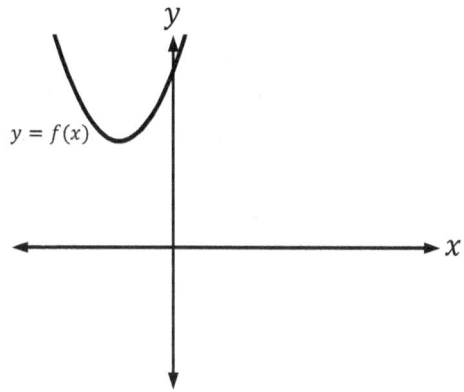

The graph shown in the xy-plane has equation $f(x) = 2x^2 - bx + 5$, where b is a constant. Which of the following is a possible value of b?

A) -1

B) 0

C) 1

D) 2

43.

$$(\sqrt[5]{x^8} \cdot \sqrt[10]{x^4})^5 = x^a$$

In the equation above, a is a constant. What is the value of a?

44.

Before the election, a town council consisting of 5 members had an average age of 57 years old. In the election, 3 members retained their positions on the town council, while 2 members were replaced. The new members on the town council are 12 and 18 years younger than the members that they replaced, respectively. What is the average age of the newly elected town council?

A) 50

B) 51

C) 52

D) 53

45.

In the xy-plane, a linear function f that intersects another linear function g at the point $(1, 2)$ also passes through the point $(7, -5)$. If the graphs of f and g are perpendicular, what is the y-intercept of the graph of g?

46.

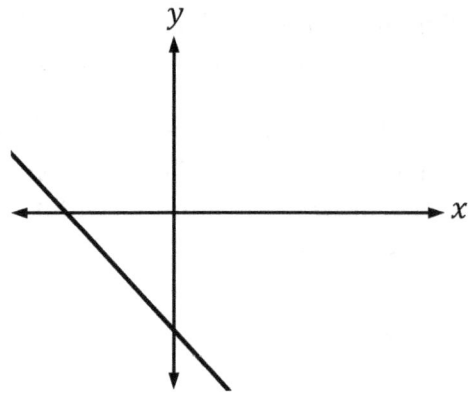

The graph of the line shown above has equation $ax + by = c$, where a, b, and c are constants. Which of the following must be true?

A) $c < 0$

B) $a > b$

C) If a is negative, then b is positive.

D) If c is negative, then a is positive.

47.

$$3x^2 - 18x + 3y^2 + 12y = 72$$

The equation above defines a circle with a radius of $\sqrt{n}$, where n is a constant. What is the value of n?

A) 18

B) 24

C) 37

D) 72

48.

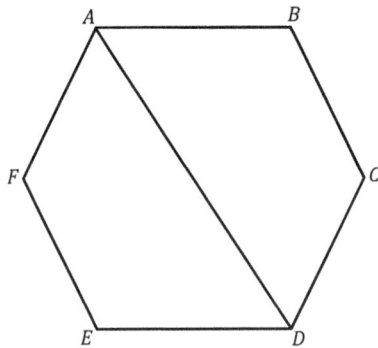

The area of the regular hexagon above is $54\sqrt{3}$. What is the length of segment $\overline{AD}$?

A) 9

B) 10

C) 11

D) 12

49.

$$\frac{x^2 + 3x - 10}{(x+5)(x+3)} - \frac{x-2}{x+3} = 0$$

How many solutions does the equation above have?

A) Zero

B) One

C) Two

D) More than two

50.

A new bakery sells two items: cookies and muffins. Both are sold in two different flavors: chocolate chip and peanut butter. One day, the probability of randomly selecting a peanut butter item is 0.30 and the probability of randomly selecting a chocolate chip cookie is 0.25. If there are 160 total bakery items to be sold on that day, how many chocolate chip muffins are there to be sold?

A) 40

B) 48

C) 64

D) 72

Answers

1. Linear Equations

1) D
2) $\frac{4}{3}$
3) 2
4) C
5) B
6) D
7) A
8) B
9) 4
10) B
11) A
12) 1
13) D
14) C
15) D
16) D
17) B
18) A
19) 6
20) B
21) 6
22) B
23) 8
24) B
25) D
26) D
27) D
28) 2
29) C
30) D
31) C
32) A
33) A
34) A
35) C
36) D
37) C
38) A
39) C
40) 2
41) A
42) C
43) $\frac{14}{3}$
44) 0
45) D
46) B
47) $\frac{17}{5}$
48) D
49) A
50) A

2. Systems of Equations

1) 7
2) C
3) 3
4) C
5) 0
6) A
7) 4
8) C
9) A
10) B
11) 2
12) B
13) 1
14) C
15) A
16) B
17) B
18) C
19) B
20) B
21) D
22) D
23) C
24) 1.5
25) D
26) 50
27) B
28) 10
29) 2

30) C

31) $\frac{1}{2}$

32) 6

33) D

34) 70

35) 16

36) D

37) B

38) A

39) $\frac{10}{7}$

40) 8

41) 2.4

42) $\frac{15}{4}$

43) B

44) A

45) 1.5

46) C

47) B

48) D

49) B

50) B

3. Quadratic Equations

1) D

2) B

3) C

4) B

5) D

6) 60

7) B

8) C

9) C

10) C

11) C

12) D

13) 40

14) 15

15) B

16) C

17) 53

18) D

19) C

20) D

21) A

22) B

23) C

24) B

25) 3

26) D

27) 25

28) 4

29) C

30) 20

31) A

32) C

33) C

34) A

35) D

36) D

37) $\frac{2}{3}$

38) B

39) C

40) A

41) 4

42) D

43) 6

44) A

45) 8

46) A

47) D

48) 1

49) D

50) 4

4. Percents

1) 78

2) A

3) 24

4) C

5) 8.5

6) 40

7) 7200

8) C

9) 26

10) C

11) A

12) B

13) 208
14) C
15) 1300
16) C
17) C
18) B
19) 297
20) D
21) B
22) 20
23) 10.1
24) B
25) B
26) B
27) .75
28) 13
29) B
30) C
31) B
32) B
33) 54
34) C
35) C
36) B
37) B
38) B
39) C
40) C
41) C
42) C
43) C
44) B
45) 55.6
46) A
47) C
48) B
49) C
50) D

5. Solving

1) C
2) D
3) D
4) D
5) A
6) D

7) B
8) 10
9) A
10) B
11) C
12) 48
13) D
14) $\frac{1}{3}$
15) D
16) D
17) 0
18) C
19) C
20) 18
21) D
22) 10
23) D
24) A
25) 3
26) D
27) B
28) A
29) B
30) D
31) A
32) C
33) A
34) 2.25
35) B
36) A
37) $\frac{1}{5}$
38) B
39) 1
40) A
41) B
42) D
43) $\frac{16}{3}$
44) 10
45) A
46) C
47) D
48) C
49) C
50) $\frac{1}{2}$

6. Exponents

1) C
2) A
3) C
4) B
5) D
6) D
7) D
8) D
9) A
10) B
11) C
12) B
13) C
14) B
15) A
16) D
17) 4
18) D
19) A
20) C
21) C
22) A
23) A
24) B
25) A
26) 5
27) B
28) D
29) B
30) B
31) C
32) B
33) D
34) 7
35) B
36) D
37) C
38) .44
39) D
40) B
41) A
42) D
43) B
44) C
45) C
46) D
47) D
48) D
49) D
50) C

7. Geometry

1) C
2) C
3) C
4) $\frac{4}{5}$
5) 60
6) A
7) 40.5
8) A
9) D
10) 10
11) B
12) A
13) B
14) C
15) 79
16) C
17) D
18) A
19) C
20) D
21) C
22) C
23) D
24) 7
25) B
26) D
27) D
28) D
29) C
30) $\frac{16}{5}$
31) C
32) C
33) D
34) C
35) 14
36) C
37) A
38) A

39) A
40) 3
41) 24
42) D
43) B
44) $\frac{5}{36}$
45) C
46) C
47) 4
48) B
49) A
50) C

8. Statistics

1) B
2) 3.91
3) D
4) B
5) B
6) B
7) D
8) C
9) C
10) C
11) C
12) C
13) B
14) B
15) C
16) D
17) A
18) D
19) .2
20) D
21) B
22) C
23) D
24) B
25) A
26) C
27) C
28) D
29) C
30) B

31) A
32) C
33) .68
34) A
35) D
36) C
37) C
38) C
39) C
40) A
41) D
42) 65
43) C
44) B
45) D
46) C
47) C
48) B
49) A
50) B

9. "Advanced" Math

1) C
2) A
3) D
4) C
5) B
6) C
7) D
8) A
9) D
10) 5
11) D
12) B
13) 300
14) C
15) D
16) C
17) .52
18) D
19) D
20) B
21) A
22) $\frac{5}{12}$

23) B
24) $\frac{2}{5}$
25) B
26) D
27) 240
28) 6
29) B
30) C
31) $\frac{2}{3}$
32) D
33) 6.5
34) D
35) D
36) A
37) B
38) D
39) 31
40) C
41) A
42) D
43) B
44) B
45) B
46) C
47) A
48) B
49) $\frac{3}{4}$
50) D

10. Final Exam

1) 17
2) D
3) 6
4) A
5) B
6) D
7) A
8) A
9) 3
10) D
11) C
12) C
13) $\frac{1}{6}$
14) 4

15) 27
16) D
17) C
18) D
19) C
20) A
21) A
22) 7
23) C
24) B
25) C
26) C
27) D
28) C
29) D
30) C
31) B
32) B
33) A
34) C
35) D
36) A
37) B
38) B
39) A
40) 570
41) D
42) A
43) 10
44) B
45) $\frac{8}{7}$
46) D
47) C
48) D
49) D
50) D